PASSAGES II

An Encore Anthology
of
Shelby County History

Albert Binkley Dickas, Ph.D.

Shelby County Historical Society
Sidney, Ohio   2014

Copyright © 2014 by Albert Binkley Dickas

All rights reserved

Published by the Shelby County Historical Society

Reproduction or translation of any part of this work beyond that permitted by Section 107 or 108 of the 1976 United States Copyright Act without the permission of the copyright owner is unlawful. Requests for permission or further information should be addressed to:

Shelby County Historical Society
PO Box 376
Sidney, Ohio 45365-0376

Book design by PenworthyLLC

Some illustrations in this book have been adapted from images used with permission from clipart.com and Getty Images.

ISBN: 0-9713477-9-4

Dedicated
to
Rachael Garrity

A Friend in Need
and
A Friend Indeed

*History is little more than the register of
the crimes, follies, and misfortunes of mankind.*

Edward Gibbon (1737-1794)

----

*History is the version of past events
that people have decided to agree upon.*

Napoleon Bonaparte (1769-1821)

----

*History is not a burden on the memory,
but an illumination of the soul.*

John Edward Dalberg-Acton (1834-1902)

History takes time.

Gertrude Stein (1874-1946)

----

*History is the sum total of things
that could have been avoided.*

Konrad Adenauer (1876-1967)

TABLE OF CONTENTS

Entrepreneurial Accomplishments
    Community of Yore _____ 3
    Fully Aged Health _____ 13
    Homemade Horseless Carriage _____ 21
    Couturier to the Celebrated _____ 29
    Moments of Fame _____ 37

Episodes of Emancipation
    Randolph's Buckeye Legacy _____ 47
    Escapes from Oppression _____ 55
    One Man's War _____ 63
    The Boys of '98 _____ 71
    Return of the Doughboys _____ 79

City & County Innovations
    Antebellum River Commerce _____ 89
    Progressive Union Projects _____ 97
    CCC Company 3526 _____ 105
    Light Up Time _____ 113
    Wings and Wheels _____ 121

Discrepancies of Humanity
    Too Big to Fail _____ 131
    Environments of Mayhem _____ 139
    Prosecution and Acquittal _____ 147
    Murder Most Mercenary _____ 155
    Effect and Cause _____ 163

Recollections of This and That
    Tales of Tawawa _____ 173
    Old Time Religion _____ 181
    Black Friday 1893 _____ 189
    Persons Once Remembered _____ 197
    Observations, Chidings and Opinions _____ 205

PASSAGES

FOREWORD

I have now been retired for almost 16 years, and my daily routine is fairly well established. Upon waking, I anticipate each new day in light of an agenda that more often than not is certain. Of course, there are those matters of routine occurrence that must be addressed: keeping the kitchen sink clean of dirty dishes, assuring a degree of cleanliness about the house, checking to see if the pantry shelves contain sufficient sustenance should the suggestion of a "wintery-mix" storm be announced by The Weather Channel and --- well, you get the idea, I am sure.

With prescribed duties completed, I am free to contemplate the already determined agenda, commonly composed of one or more activities: travel, reading and writing. The ideal is combining all three into an extended project, one in which I review a collection of books in preparation for a visit to an unfamiliar corner of the world and then, upon return to my home base, I incorporate the experiences and new-found information into an essay.

PASSAGES: An Anthology of Shelby County History, published through the Shelby County Historical Society, is the product of one of those combined and extended projects. When that volume was completed in 2013, I thought I had satisfied my curiosity regarding all those items of history that related to the years during, and before, the period of time I was growing up in Sidney. No sooner had a copy of *PASSAGES* been placed within my library, however, than I realized I was wrong. There was more to do.

In writing *PASSAGES II: An Encore Anthology of Shelby County History*, I began with travel -- a journey into my past and the determination of 25 topics of interest associated with the city and county of my youth. Routine was easily established: periodic travel north to Sidney followed by day(s)-long confinement in the basement of Amos Memorial Library viewing microfilm records of the excellent collection of community-based newspapers. When I returned to my home in Virginia, I had to collate, arrange and condense the pages of collected information. During this phase, I scanned the files and web pages of the Shelby County Historical Society for purposes of verifying facts and discovering new tidbits of information. Within these founts of history, the two volumes written by Richard Wallace and published in 2001 and 2003 -- *Voices from the Past* and *Voices from the Past, Volume II* -- were of particular value.

In several instances topics covered in the *Voices from the Past* volumes are revisited in *PASSAGES II*. Examples include the saga of the Randolph slaves, stories of Tawawa Park, the career of Herman Tappe and episodes involving Whistling Joe Gutman, Alfred Artis and Buddie Shang. In each case, I took care to be sure that *PASSAGES II* was written from a differing perspective or that it contained information not previously recorded.

This yearlong project has given me a deep sense of fulfillment. My hope is it will be considered of lasting value to the better understanding of Shelby County history.

Albert Binkley Dickas
Brush Mountain, Virginia
March 2014

PASSAGES II

An Encore Anthology
of
Shelby County History

ENTREPRENEURIAL ACCOMPLISHMENTS

Years ago, a study of the "merits" or "values" of a group of senior members of the faculty of a prestigious US university -- all having been on campus for at least two decades, all tenured, and all expected to achieve enough recognition in their respective fields to improve the reputation of the university and even advance humanity -- revealed they could be divided into three groups. Fifteen percent were academic leaders "par excellence" with Nobel Prize potential. Fifteen percent were associated with a time-worn suggestion: "Those who give by the inch and take by the yard should be kicked by the foot." The remaining seventy percent were listed as yeomen of their trade – dutiful to the task but generally lacking in resolve and ambition. The authors of the study concuded that any chosen group of persons would most likely reveal the same: individuals good, bad and indifferent.

Certainly, Shelby County history includes persons in the "par excellence" category – they made things happen, and helped to produce a better world, at least at the local level. Their careers involved the creation of spirits, automobiles, fashion and entertainment, accomplishments probably not possible had they not worked in a community already established and on the move.

Two nostalgic reviews of that "older Sidney" exist. The first outlines the community in the year 1855 through the eyes of a 12-year-old girl. The second begins in the wilderness year of 1819 and ends some half-century later when America is slowly recovering from the devastating effects of a Civil War.

ALBERT DICKAS

COMMUNITY OF YORE

Histories are composed by the gathering and conglomeration of many different aspects of information: personal remembrances, recorded tidbits, treasured letters, miscellaneous oddities, familial gossip and the ever-present odd bits of fact and fiction. Two such historical accounts are given here, in their original and unvarnished form, as published in *The Sidney Journal* and the *Sidney Daily News*.

The first, from the April 29, 1919 issue of the *Sidney Daily News*, looks back to the pre-Civil War community of 1855, when the Valley City was only 35 years old.

REMINISCENCES OF OLD SIDNEY

After an absence of sixty-four years, Mrs. C. M. Deming, of Kansas City, realized the desire she had to see the home of her girlhood and came to Sidney to spend several days, stopping at the Wagner hotel.

Mrs. Deming is a daughter of William Girard, who was a prominent contractor in Sidney at that time building many of the old houses and buildings around the city. She remembers particularly of his erecting the building where Christian's Drug Store and Kraft's Shoe Store is now located. The family home was on south Walnut avenue with the two story shop to the north, while where Klipstine's Lumber Company buildings now are her father had his lumber kiln;

for the carpenters in those days did all the work connected with preparing the wood, cutting the timber, sawing, drying the wood and making all the doors and sash.

Her father's old shop was one of the first buildings that her eyes rested upon, as it had been moved to this side of the canal and is now located at West avenue and Poplar street and is used by Sidney Marble and Granite works. She said it seemed as if she could see the men working at the benches in the shop so vivid were her impressions.

Mr. Girard lost his property in (sic) the old Dayton and Michigan railroad, which is now the B. & O. road and moved with his family to Iowa. She remembers the building of the New York Central through Sidney, then called the Bellefontaine and Indiana railroad and how the first train came thundering in. Her father put up several buildings for the founder of Pemberton and they became great friends. It was a great day when the Girard family went over to Pemberton for an over Sunday visit and thus she had her first car ride. The noise of the train frightened her and she was afraid someone was being killed.

Mrs. Deming attended the M. E. church on Sunday and sat beside her childhood friend, Mrs. Lou Frazer Horr, and thought of the times that they had gone as children to the old frame church which stood where the Baptist church now stands. She is named for Mrs. Horrs' mother, Mrs. J. F. Frazer, and aunt, Mrs. Frankenberger, Nancy Caroline. She thought the old brick court house very fine when a child and the stone jail was in the southeast corner of the square. She was a friend of the jailor's daughter by name of France and she was allowed to see a colored man, a murderer, a few days before he was to be executed. The Baptist minister was with him at the time and she remembers the minister saying to him that he was soon to appear before the bar of God. Mr. and Mrs. McGooken had a private school on Popular street at that time while Mr. Pampel had two rooms fitted up in the second story in the north part of what is now the Heiser building, the other part being used as a factory. The older scholars were taught by Mr. Pampel while Miss Martha Crowell was her teacher. On their way to school the children crossed the old stone bridge, but when the canal boats were unloading at the warehouse by the bridge the children would go the long way round to school being afraid of the boatman who would call to them and would be swearing as they were unloading. There was a covered market house on East Poplar street between Main and Miami avenue with room for driving on each side. Here market was held three times a week and it was a great pleasure for the children to get up early in the morning and go to market with their father.

The cholera was an epidemic in Sidney for a year or so a short time before the Girard family left and people were very much afraid of it and would not go near them but her parents were not and would go where it was and help. An aunt, Mrs. DeLapp, was taken ill one night and died the next morning, while an uncle, David Carey, who was one of the Carey brothers of the pioneer family of Sidney, lingered for two weeks and they had great hopes of his recovery.

Mrs. Deming, although seventy-six years of age, is as bright and active as a woman much younger in years and is fully enjoying her visit to the city of her birth.

The second history was read before the Progressive Union by Mrs. E. H. Arbuckle, on Monday evening, July 10, 1893. It was published four days later on the front page of the regular Friday edition of *The Sidney Journal*.

OLD SIDNEY

In our journey through life we may find it interesting and beneficial to take a retrospective glance at the paths already gone over by our fathers. Sidney, in its infancy and growth up to the present time, has not made rapid strides, but we think good ones, and the energy of its people is apparent everywhere. When the pioneers of our country chose the spot where we now dwell, they chose wisely, although they knew not how good a choice they had made. The poet has not written of its charms, nor has the artist fully portrayed its beauties on canvas, yet our place is unrivaled for its charming location, and quite romantic enough to please the most fastidious eye. We view the town with a just pride as it stands today down in the valley among the hills which border on the Great Miami river, with it buildings and homes of every kind bearing the stamp of improvement and happiness.

In the fall of 1819 Charles Starrett gave 70 acres to the county, with the proviso that the seat of justice be permanently located in Sidney. One acre was to be reserved for a public square, two half acres for two religious societies, two acres for cemetery use of said societies, and one acre for school purposes. For the advancement of the same object there were others who made contributions of cash, or work, or goods, the whole amounting to about $690. The Court directed the county seat to be removed from Hardin to Sidney in April, 1820, and the history of the town, we may say, commenced with this date, although there were scattered cabins to be found previous to that time. The only part of the plat cleared was a corn field, the first crop having been raised there in 1809 by William Stewart, after the ground had been procured from an Indian tribe, and where tradition proclaims had been the home of Indian Princes, and the place where the assembled Nations had met to enjoy feasting and smoke the pipe of peace, or sing the war song, and where was left only the moldering vestiges of their former glory. Sidney was named after Sir Philip Sydney, who, the exponent of courtly grace, was a brilliant ornament of the court of Queen Elizabeth. East Sidney, embracing the old site of Dingmansburg, was surveyed and made a part of the town proper in 1837. This plat was surveyed by Joel Frankeberger and John F. Frazier, but for some reason, not on the records, the town had been platted and located almost 15 years before it was incorporated. The first court was held in 1820, in the log cabin of Abraham Cannon, on the south side of lot 49. During the same year the first court house was built, a frame building 24 by 30 feet, which was used afterward by Judge Walker for a store on the lot where now stands the brick dwelling house owned by Mrs. Mary Barkdall. The jail, built of logs, was 16 by 18 feet, and when a jail bird escaped the Commissioners were obliged to pay the fine for the nonpayment of which the prisoner was confined. In 1832 a brick structure, 44 feet square and two stories high, was erected in the center of the public square for a court house. This building, with its numerous windows for light -- 16 in number below and 20 above -- an entrance door in each of its four facings, its outside walls painted and penciled, and a shingle roof, and its crowning ornament, the steeple, fashioned like a pepper castor, was considered an additional beauty to the town.

October 24, 1842, the log jail was discovered on fire, and burnt all day until consumed. Two men confined there had set it on fire to make sure their escape, and thus gave opportunity for another improvement. There were no trees in the square at this date, but there were stumps large and small for ornament, else for stumbling blocks to a dark night, in case the passerby thought to mail a letter and had neglected to bring his lantern. James Wells was allowed the privilege of keeping the first postoffice in the court house, paying the sum of $3 in compensation for the use of the room for one year.

In June, 1839, a few of the residents of public spirit, desiring to improve the appearance of the square, and hoping to keep the stray cattle from making a resting place of the ground, took a subscription, and a contract was let at $329.25 to Samuel Mathers for fencing the same, but in 1840 the Commissioners of the county sold out the tearing down of this fence, and intended building another 50 feet off, of octagon form. An injunction was taken and sustained that the county had no right to the square, nor had they any right to occupy and build thereon. The court house and square, in early days, were used for different purposes, for on June 3, 1841, the women of the Presbyterian congregation held the first fair there, and received for benevolent purposes $75, also in the same year a Fourth of July celebration was held. A large crowd met in the court house, formed a procession in the square, and marched with music to the Methodist meeting house, and, after services of prayer by the Rev. Bair, singing by the people, and an oration by J. S. Conklin, they returned in the same order, and the whole crowd partook of a bounteous dinner, served under a bower which had been prepared by Adam Werst.

One of the steps taken by those in authority was the location of the *public roads. They marked out the main road from Piqua through to Wapakoneta, and from this as a starting point traced through the forest as best they could for a passable route to other points they desired to reach. The pike system, now so complete, was little dreamed of by the first surveyors.*

The first frame dwelling house built in 1820 was on lot 49, said lot purchased for $125 by John Blake and was considered the finest house to be found for miles around. Mr. Blake petitioned the Court for license to keep tavern in 1825, and in consideration of the payment of $5 for one year it was granted. The same building was sold to J. W. Carey, who made noteworthy improvements, and a handsomely painted sign was put out to tell the weary traveler here was a resting place, and good board could be obtained for $1.25 a week. This house changed owners until it came into possession of Matthias Wagner, and the lot, with its new handsome brick structure, is still owned by his heirs. The first brick dwelling house was built by Dr. William Fielding, afterward used by J. F. Frazer for a drug store, and stood on the rear of the lot where Piper Brothers are now erecting a new building.

No material embarrassment among the early settlers was permitted to obscure the thought of their spiritual welfare, and as early as 1820 a missionary effort was made to establish a congregation. A little band of people, by a request of the Rev. Joseph Stevenson, met in the old court house and formed into a congregation called the Presbyterian. Of that little band, so earnest in its desires and so zealous in promoting the cause of Christianity, there remains today but one -- Mrs. Elizabeth Fielding. The first house of worship cost about $900, and stood on the rear of the lot where now stands the building completed in 1882. The Associate (now called United Presbyterian) church formed a congregation in 1829. The Rev. John Reynolds was a supply for a time, until it built on the rear of the lot where now stands the German Lutheran church building. There are not any of the original members living. The first Methodist association held services occasionally in the court house prior to 1850, later in the Union Hall, until it occupied the old Methodist church building, and on the spot where it stood it has recently built and dedicated its own house of worship. The Catholics were few in number in 1848, and assembled in private houses for worship. The missionary spirit manifested itself among the few German Lutherans and German reformed believers at an early day, and while they did not forget their denominational attachments, they were active in their efforts to disseminate the truth.

The religious training of the young was carefully considered, and, while the secular school gave special attention to the reading of the Scriptures, the Sunday school was an early organization, and as Sunday school literature has grown to be an important department of religious literature only in the last three decades, there were not the newspaper and the library book to read and fascinate the mind, but the memorizing of the Scripture and the catechism and the reciting of them to teacher, were the work of the scholar in the early Sunday school.

We may say the educational spirit of the pioneers was intense. They did not come to their uncultivated lands simply to reap a fortune. Some of them brought with them learning and wisdom and culture from the homes they left, and while with willing hearts and hands for the work before them they tilled the soil and sowed the seed and reaped the harvest as it came, they had an appreciation of the value of education, and one of their first desires was to establish schools. Private schools were taught previous to 1841. The Rev. Samuel Cleland, Mr. Maltby and several others were good schoolmasters, and we have the testimony that boys and young men who afterward took a collegiate course had been well prepared under these early instructors, both in the English and Latin. In 1841 four free schools were established and supported from a fund. A. Lynch, Abraham Fulton, Alexander Green and one other were paid $75 a quarter. As the years passed schools improved and education became more general, and while the curriculum would now be considered simple, the instruction received served as a foundation for the future and gave a moral atmosphere to their surroundings. Among the pupils who received their early day lessons in some one of the old log or frame school houses we mention Mrs. M. Burgess, of Washington city, the Rev. James Marshall, the Rev. Finley Hutchison, Judge Ewing Bailey and R. D. Marshall, of other cities, beside many of *our town's most worthy residents. In 1857, after a strife with regard to location, the Union school building was erected, and for years was the pride of the town. The first Superintendent was the Rev. Joseph Shaw. His salary was $800 for the year, and with the assistance of his efficient corps of teachers, he was successful. The second Superintendent, Ira W. Allen, taught by example the precepts he wished instilled in the hands of the pupils. Careful and polite in his manners and chaste in language, he was called Lord Chesterfield. There were many successful Superintendents, and the pupils of the first Union school are now filling places of honor and trust, both in Sidney and abroad. Dr. W. J. Conklin, of Dayton; Judge McPherson, of Pennsylvania, and Clara Conklin, Professor of Languages in Wesleyan University, Delaware, were students in this school.*

For the first 20 years the town's growth kept along apace with that of the county. In 1839 an agricultural society was formed, and the first county fair was held in October of the same year. A premium list amounting to $45 was prepared, and the fair was considered a success. Of the officers of that association there is but one person living at the present time -- William Murphey.

We find from the records that steps were taken very early for establishing such business as the times seemed to demand. The merchant, the grocer, the shoemaker, and the cabinetmaker were represented, as well as all classes of professional men. In the spring of 1840 there were 11 merchants, of whom there are none now living; three grocers, of whom Guy C. Kelsey is still a resident of Sidney; there were seven physicians, of whom Dr. P Beeman is still here; five lawyers, of whom there are none remaining; four blacksmiths, four carpenters, bricklayers and plasterers numbered five; there were two tanneries, four cabinetmakers, two grist mills, three tailors. We must not omit the one editor and printer, and the loafers and tattlers were numerous in a population of 700.

During the years of 1837-39 the canal fever was raging, and public sentiment was keenly awakened to the belief that a canal would be an improvement and a benefit to the town. At least there would be a more agreeable mode of transit on the packet than in the lumbering stage coach, which was the customary mode of travel for business men going to Dayton to deposit in bank or for purchasing goods in Cincinnati, but it was not until 1843 that the first boat arrived from Piqua with a volunteer company on board to celebrate the occasion, and fully a year after until the canal was in order to carry freight. It is within the recollection of some of our residents that in July, 1846, quite a commotion was caused in the village by the arrival of a boat carrying as passengers Judge Lee, of Kentucky, and about 100 Randolph slaves, just set free. The boat passed through up to the vicinity of Berlin, but the Negroes were not allowed to land. A mob received them with sticks and stones: they met a like reception when a part of them, on their return, attempted to stop off here. Finally Judge Lee appealed to the charity of the town, and left them in an old building where now stands Mr. Musselman's livery stable. Immediately a meeting was called in the Council room in the old Carey Hotel. There were present at the meeting Dr. Thomas, Gay C. Kelsey, William Murphey, Joseph Updegraft, Joseph Cummins, and doubtless others whose names are not recalled. The decision was to send them around to different localities. Some of them went to Piqua, and others north of Sidney. It was the exclamation of one of the old Negroes that he guessed his "Master was his first friend, after all."

One enterprise, which, although it did not meet with the success desired, is worthy of mention. As early as 1869 the first public library came into existence. It cost less than $100, but after the books had been read over a number of times they were sold at auction at a loss of about 331/3 percent. In the year 1832 a diminutive newspaper made its appearance. It did not contain much of an editorial, and but few locals, yet it chronicled events as they could be obtained from travelers who came and went in the weekly stage coach. Mr. Smith was the editor of this paper. In August, 1839, a Whig paper, called the Aurora, was issued by Mr. Stout.

In 1852 there was great rejoicing over the completion of the railway to Bellefontaine -- a free ride and a free dinner to those who went. The building of the Dayton and Michigan railway commenced in 1855; was not completed for several years. There was a heavy drain made on the people, and money, town lots, houses and everything which could be turned into railway stock was given, but the crisis passed, and Sidney today is reaping the benefit of the steps taken which seemed likely to cause financial disaster to the early projectors of the movement.

Party spirit ran high among the old residents, both Whig and Democrats holding on to their opinions with tenacity. No more exciting time ever was known than that of the summer and fall of 1840, and we notice the complaints of one party against the other were about as pertinent as those brought forward today by one politician against another.

It would be almost impossible to note all improvements as they were made from time to time. The tearing down of old buildings and the putting up of new ones, the changing of roads and streets for convenience, etc. To gather up the memories of all these days, and to speak of the lives, the customs and the familiar events of the past and passing generations, would furnish material for a history.

In closing this imperfect review, what a comparison we might make between now and 60 years ago: and what would be the decision? We think each one of you would say, that while you desire to preserve the memories of our noble ancestors, who have worthily served their time and generation, and while it is with a sincere pride you view the results of their efforts, yet the needs of that day would not satisfy the wishes of today: the homes and houses, the church and school buildings of olden times, would not be suitable for the people of modern times. Let us hope that the spirit of improvement which was manifested in our forefathers may be inculcated in us in accordance with the superior advantages which we have over that day, and thus, under a wise government, guided by a Divine ruler, our village may become a city more wise, more beautiful and more prosperous than any of the famous world cities which have preceded it in the long march of centuries.

FULLY AGED HEALTH

By the year 1850 the population of Sidney was rapidly growing. It was a village with great potential, because of its strategic location along a navigable south-flowing river that gave it ready access to Cincinnati. One of the many new faces seen around town was that of 16-year-old John Wagner, who two years before had arrived with his parents from Columbiana County, his place of birth. Growing in stature and learning the rudiments of arithmetic and penmanship from Judge N. R. Wyman, who taught school in the evening, he worked in the butchering business for a few years with his brother Mathias. With the belief, perhaps, that illumination was just as important as sustenance to the average person, he established a tallow candle factory on the northwest corner of Ohio Avenue and West Court Street. Failing in that endeavor, he returned to the butcher business, a vocation that eventually led to the establishment of his own meat market.

Climbing the ladder of success, John married Mary Meyer of Sidney on January 26, 1858, and soon thereafter leased the brewery built by his other brother, Joseph, in 1850. That arrangement was subsequently altered when, with yet another brother, Peter, he purchased an interest in the enterprise. Seventeen years later he assumed sole proprietorship, enlarged the facility and began to manufacture a popular style of beer that had been brought to the United States from Western Europe in 1846. Branded with the family name, it became "Wagner's Golden Lager." By 1880 the mention of John Wagner was synonymous with beer in Sidney and the surrounding country. One year later, on May 1, he died at the age of 46 years, 6 months and 16 days.

The *Shelby County Democrat* eulogized him as "a man of quiet and moderate demeanor, who never intruded himself on anyone, yet there was no man in the county to whom more persons went for counsel than to him, and there was none prepared to give better business counsel than he was." Described by William Binkley in *The Sidney Journal* as "slow in speech, but always to the point," he was already one of Sidney's most enterprising citizens. Following services conducted in Holy Angels church by the Reverend Father F. M. Quatman, he was carried to rest by ten pallbearers chosen from a list of prominent Sidney families: W. C. Wyman, William Shine, John Heiser, Christ Kingseed, the brothers Joseph and Louis Winegartner, George Hemm, Christopher H. Dickas, H. M. Lehman and Joseph Allenbaugh.

In 1896 the beer-making facility was incorporated as The John Wagner Sons Brewing Company, a family-owned enterprise managed by the founders three sons; Henry, Edward and Louis. Their mother, Mrs. Mary Wagner, occupied the office of president, while Henry functioned as vice-president and Edward acted in the capacity of secretary and treasurer. When Sidney held its first Labor Day parade three years later, the colorful brewery float was manned by 20 employees, each wearing a company-furnished blue working blouse displaying a badge inscribed "Our Day." For purposes long forgotten, each man also carried an umbrella, symbolic perhaps of the fact the Wagner enterprise was by then undergoing a "storm of production activity," as indeed it was.

By the beginning of the teen-decade of the 20th century, the outlook for the Sidney hops and malt business appeared ever brighter. The plant covered a full acre of ground and was equipped with cutting-edge equipment. The cellars had a storage capacity of 28,000 barrels of Golden Pilsener Lager in addition to vast quantities of bottled Pale American Export, enough to supply regional thirst requirements for more than a year. Then the unthinkable happened, a one-two punch that over the next half dozen years drastically altered the economic bottom line of the East Poplar Street factory.

For days the newspaper reports had been monitoring storms of whirlwind intensity that were sweeping the south and west. The weather front was moving northeastward across the Great Plains, into Ohio and the Great Lakes region. Accompanied by snow, sleet and hail, the torrential onslaught was described as the most destructive of the year and one rarely equaled in the extent of its sweep and damage.

Tuesday, March 25, 1913, dawned to a city in full-flood mode. The bloated waters of the Great Miami River extended from Brooklyn Avenue in the east to Miami Avenue in the west, the highest ever recorded in the recollections of the old-timers. Turgid currents swirled over East Court Street and reached the second floor level of Wagner's Brewery. Encouraged by a large crowd, O. S. Kenney launched his boat on East Popular Street near the flooded brewery in an attempt to rescue the Singer family, a feat finally accomplished with more than a dash of bravery. By 2 o'clock the next day, the river level had receded almost five feet and the worst was over, but it would be some time before beer production levels would again be normal.

Six years later, a 104-word, two-paragraph, notice on the inside page of the May 17 issue of the *Sidney Daily News* announced the approach of an event that would decidedly change life both locally and nationally. Beer, the well-known, readily available beverage, touted by many a watering-hole habitue as salubrious and possibly medicinal, would soon be taken off the market. In effect, "Shelby County will be dry after next Saturday." Throughout the state, the doors of 5,000 saloons were closed. Prohibition was now the law of the land.

Around the public square the saloons did a landmark business that memorable day, one proprietor reporting total sales in excess of $1,800. The Sidney police department announced the death of "Old John Barleycorn" took place with "a fewer number of drunks reported" and "only three arrests being made during the entire day for intoxication." By 6 o'clock a mere handful of bars were still open, all the others having been closed due to the sale of their entire stock. The White Front locked its doors three hours later, and the Wagner House Annex followed shortly. Late night revelers found the Palmisano saloon in the Metropole Hotel and Keplinger's place on West Poplar Street the only taverns left open.

New businesses began to move into the vacant rooms as soon as the odors of stale beer had been dissipated. The White Front became an outlet for the Chickering Company, purveyors of pianos and harpsichords. John Steinle said the Elks Café was now a restaurant and soft drink establishment. William Bauer, not wishing to be left without income, made a similar announcement. Down on East Poplar Street, Edward Wagner assembled the Board of Directors -- a new business plan obviously had to be developed.

The discussions could not have been overly contentious, because the need was quite obvious; retool or cease to operate. Across the nation brewery personnel were examining ways to modify the equipment of beer manufacturing to that of "soda pop" production. The Wagner facility could convert its operation, of course, but there was the Cherry Cheer Company to consider. "Made from genuine cherry . . . not a wild cherry or an artificial flavor . . . an agreeable tang that everyone likes," Cherry Cheer was first manufactured in 1907 in the form of fountain syrup in the basement of Wilson Carothers' home on Walnut Avenue. Success was immediate and by the end of World War I the company, having moved into the vacated Underwood Whip Company building, was bottling and distributing a soft drink, in addition to making a line of fine chocolates and other "six-cent and penny dainties."

Apparently the Wagner family thought there was room in western Ohio for another non-intoxicating liquid refreshment and thus approved a July 1919 newspaper advertisement announcing a new drink: "Healthful -- Refreshing -- On Draught July 4th -- In Bottles July 11th -- Pale American Beverage," bottled by the Wagner Beverage Company. Introducing Edward J. Wagner as the proprietor of the renamed company, the publicity release was a fine example of hype and hope:

> *Realizing that the 'best is none too good' for a Sidney product, and desiring to meet the demand for a strictly high grade non-alcoholic product different from the average product of this character, a careful and painstaking investigation of the various processes of manufacturing non alcoholic beverages was made, extensive experiments were made, and it was finally decided to adopt the present method which is the one in use by many of the largest manufacturers in the country, and it is believed that the beverage*

produced will be found the best of all soft drinks and that its clean, appetizing taste and appearance will make it preferable to any soft drink on the market.

The new operation succeeded for several years, but by 1931 the hum of equipment had been silenced and some of the interior space was being used for the storage of vehicles and other equipment used by both the Platvoet Brothers and Sidney Truck and Storage in their respective businesses. Then, late in November, fire was discovered in the rear of the brick building once used as an ice plant. The entire inventory of city fire-fighting equipment was eventually brought to the scene and after two hours the situation was brought under control. The boiler house was badly damaged and the interiors of two other structures were completely gutted. In a statement to the press, Edward Wagner said he had been through the building "only a few minutes before the fire . . . and everything seemed to be all right at that time." It was time for another family meeting.

From the very beginning, any and all attempts to enforce the intentions of the 18th Amendment of the United States Constitution -- in effect, the voiding of the business license of every brewer, distiller, vintner, wholesaler and retailer of alcoholic beverages in the United States -- had resulted in failure. In the hearts and minds of many law-abiding citizens the seriously flawed legislation lacked legitimacy, and Franklin Delano Roosevelt, the newly elected 32nd President of the United States, had reason to agree. At 6:55 PM, December 5, 1933, with a flourish and a smile, he added his signature to Presidential Proclamation Order #2065, also known as the 21st Amendment of the United States Constitution. With this simple gesture the 18th Amendment was repealed and the 13-year-long alcoholic drought known as Prohibition came to an end. As legend has it, the President turned to several of his top aides and said, "I believe this would be a good time for a beer."

Down on East Poplar Street Edward Wagner started the ball rolling -- or should it be said, started the barrel rolling? Stockholders were identified, plans drawn, equipment ordered and the first of an estimated future workforce of more than 500 persons hired. As the autumn winds of 1935 began to blow across the floodplain of the Great Miami River, Edward, president of The John Wagner Company Brewery, and his selected vice-president and general manager, F. E. Wanamaker, announced the arrival of ten rail carloads of machinery from the Frick Company of Waynesboro, Pennsylvania, and more than forty truckloads of material from Littleford Brothers of Cincinnati.

When the doors were formally opened in April of 1936, thousands of guests from Sidney and the surrounding communities were heard to express opinions that ranged from "unbelievable" to "outstanding." The fact that everyone was offered a free luncheon and a glass of "that Old time Wagner Beer, fully aged, full flavored with its own superb bouquet and aroma" in all probability added to the positive slant of the evaluations. Modernization of the facility had been completed months before, but at the insistence of Brewmaster Charles Klink, a graduate of the United States Academy for Brewing in New York, the first batches of beer had to be properly aged in pitch-lined barrels before the end product could be sold. Already the volume of aged beer had been reduced significantly due to the fact that two days before a convoy of trucks had begun to distribute kegs to bars and saloons as distant as Marion, Van Wert and Hamilton. In August and September bottling and labeling equipment sufficient to produce 120 bottles of beer per minute was installed on the second floor. The renovated Wagner plant was now complete, a model front-to-aft operation that ranged from input of raw material to output of finished product. With pride, the management announced they were receiving "A constant demand . . . from the surrounding states as well as from nearly every county in the State of Ohio" on a steady basis.

Unfortunately the sense of euphoria did not last long. In 1938 the company was placed in receivership by Judge D. F. Mills, following receipt of a $1,657.68 bill for coal from the Peoples Fuel and Supply Company. Other creditors were listed in the court records, F. E. Wanamaker and the estate of E. J. Wagner being two of the many.

Today, 75 years after the John Wagner Brewery fell into receivership, only a handful of individuals who can recall the fulfilling satisfaction of quaffing a frosty bottle of Wagner's Old Time beer on a muggy summer afternoon are still alive. In time even the brewing formula for this one-time advertised "fully aged health" concoction will sadly be lost to history. Fortunately, however, the drinking public is left with one wistful and lasting relic of the time. The lengthy advertisement of 1936, announcing the beginning of a new era of brewing in Sidney, ended with a recipe for Welsh Rarebit endorsed by the one and only Miss Julia Norwood, director of the Modern Science Institute of Toledo, Ohio:

> *One-half pint of beer (preferably Wagner's "Old Time" style), one fourth teaspoon of pepper, one teaspoon dry mustard, one tablespoon Worchester sauce, one eighth teaspoon cayenne pepper, one-half teaspoon salt, and one and one-half pounds of cut up soft yellow cheese.*
>
> *Heat everything except the cheese in a double boiler or in a chafing dish or pan over hot water. When very hot add the cheese and stir the mixture until it becomes creamy. Serve at once on toast or crackers.*

HOMEMADE HORSELESS CARRIAGE

In the mid-1800s, travel during any day of the week to Sidney from the extremities of Shelby County was an undertaking that required careful planning. The family horse had to be fed and harnessed to the carriage, the condition of the roads taken into consideration and the average time in traveling from farmyard to public square and back added to the equation, which for the typical horse was around four hours. In short, such an undertaking consumed the better part of a sunlit day and, if the road was muddy, even longer.

For many a rural family, Saturday was the time to go to town. This was the day to gather and gossip and to barter and buy, a day of anticipation and relief from the daily routine of farm chores. For a trip on a weekly basis, however, time and distance took its toll, not only on Old Dobbin, but also on the carriage. Now and then a spoke would break, a cushion rip or a wheel fall off. Normally this was a problem, but not so much for the residents of Shelby County, since Sidney was at the time home to several wagon and carriage repairers and manufacturers. Piper Wagon Works was located at 824 West Court Street. When the Rupert Wagon Shop, operating out of facilities on West Poplar Street, failed, it was taken over by Miller and Smith, makers of fine carriages. Each of these companies deserves a footnote in the industrial history of the Valley City, but with mention of the surname Bimel a multiple-page review is in order.

The Old World patriarch of the Bimel family was a tailor living in the German state of Bayern. Troubled perhaps by the slowing of the Industrial Revolution, overpopulation and agricultural reform, he gathered his wife and son, Lawrence, and looked to the New World. Landing in America, the family crossed the Appalachian Mountains and settled in Wapakoneta at the very time white settlers there were replacing the native Shawnee and Seneca populations, then being relocated westward through the Indian Removal Act of 1830. Lawrence learned the blacksmith trade, moved to Sidney in 1844, married Elizabeth Seitz, a fellow immigrant, and established the Bimel Buggy Company, maker of the "Storm King," a carriage built to survive the rigors of a northern winter. Their firstborn child, William, arrived in 1851. When the buggy venture failed because an employee stole all of the company tools and equipment, Lawrence moved the family to St. Marys and started anew with an operation named "Bimel Spoke Works." In 1861, a second son, Frederick John, was born. Eleven years later, after fire destroyed the spoke works, disaster was turned to enterprise when the factory was rebuilt under the name Bimel Spoke and Wagon Works. A satellite plant, constructed in 1879 in Portland, Indiana, made a variety of spokes, hubs and then later added automobile wheels. Lawrence died in 1888, at 61, recognized throughout west-central Ohio as a leading industrialist and a pioneer in the wagon and carriage business.

At the age of 17, William was designated superintendent of the paint department at the Bimel Spoke Works in St. Marys. Six years later, having established his reputation, he married Carrie Bradley, the daughter of a local physician. Three daughters, Gertrude, Emma and Marguarite, were born from this union. In 1888, on the death of his father, William assumed the position of chief executive officer of the Bimel Spoke and Wagon Works in St. Marys, but three years later he became its general manager when he turned the operation into a stock company. After fire destroyed the facilities of the Sidney-based American Wheel Company in 1897, a search committee approached William with offer of a trained work force and the use of a brand new $100,000 building if he would relocate. He considered this an opportunity too good to decline and moved the St. Marys operation to Sidney, where buggy bodies were made with wheels furnished by the Indiana plant. The Bimel Buggy Works thus entered the new century as a continuing operation, until August of 1904, when Sidney was shocked by the collapse of the German American Bank. The Bimel Works, one of many local businesses this failure affected, was thrown into bankruptcy and the property sold at public auction. Having died in 1901, William was thus spared knowledge of this tragedy.

One year after being named manager of the Bimel and Son plant in Portland, Frederick John married Margaret G. Kelsey, a native of St. Marys. Of their seven children, five grew to adulthood: Carl, Lelia, Hazel, Bernice and Frederick, Jr. Upon the death of his father in 1912, Carl assumed control of the family enterprise. His marriage to Louine Miller one year later was eventually blessed with one child, Carl, Jr.

Following the bankruptcy of the Sidney Bimel Buggy Works, a receiver was named to find tenants for the four-story high, brick, North Miami Avenue property. After an effecient search that ended a mere 12 months after the date of bankruptcy, a *Sidney Daily News* headline announced: "The New Bimel Buggy Company. . . an Organization Perfected to Operate the Old Bimel Carriage Company's Plant." New management, imported from Fort Wayne, Indiana, proudly announced it would resume the manufacture of "buggies and carriages and a full line of vehicles. . .keeping in mind the reputation of Bimel vehicles for good quality." Mr. G. W. Maxwell became President and Thomas Milo Miller, a former school principal, was named Vice President of Sales, assisted by six traveling salesmen.

While prospects were bright for the reorganized business, times were indeed changing. History records the first motor-driven vehicle built in America was an ordinary buggy equipped with a four-horsepower, single-cylinder engine, a rinky-dink contrivance constructed in 1893 by Charles and Frank Duryea. Ransom Olds, of Oldsmobile fame, introduced mass production technology around the turn of the century, but Henry Ford perfected the process when he sold America on the merits of the 1908 Model T, advertised as the first affordable automobile at a cost of $850. The success of the "Tin Lizzie" was a national phenomenon. With a Model T coming off the assembly line every 93 minutes, the costs had been reduced to less than $275 by the 1920s.

In the years before the beginning of World War I, advancements in automobile technologies were extensive, partly because hundreds of manufacturers were competing to gain the attention of the American consumer. In 1915 alone, mainstream manufacturers planned more than 20 new models inclusive of an armored car offered by the Maxwell Motor Company of Detroit, Michigan. This was also the year transcontinental telephone service was inaugurated, 25,000 women marched in New York City to demand the right to vote, the Ford Motor Company manufactured one million Model T automobiles and the Bimal Buggy Company decided its corporate image was due a facelift.

For years the horse-drawn carriage had put dollars into the pockets of its many investors, but with America firmly entrenched in its growing love affair with the internal combustion engine, perhaps it was time for the Bimel Company to expand its base of operation and manufacture a new product – the horseless kind. With minimal fanfare, the *Sidney Daily News* published the specifications of a Bimel five-passenger, light touring car in mid-February, 1915. Built of thoroughly tested parts on a 102-inch wheel base, driven by a four-cylinder engine fed from a 10-gallon gasoline tank and complete with a pressed steel, streamlined body supplied by the Sidney Manufacturing Company, the "Elco 30" could be bought at the factory for an even $500, or purchased at a network of dealers located throughout the United States.

The design of the Elco 30 automobile had its genesis in the small town of Elwood, Indiana, 30 miles northeast of Indianapolis. Specifics regarding the move to Sidney remain murky, but it seems Carl Bimel, son of Frederick and the manager of the Portland, Indiana, factory, bought the rights of the Elco 30, originally labeled the "Elco Four," from the Elwood Iron Works, a wannabe manufacturer that had gone bankrupt after developing a prototype vehicle, the 8-cylinder "Bailey-Klapp."

Soon the Bimel Buggy Company publicity department was cranking out various news items for whoever would secure them in printers ink: a Sidney baseball team was completely equipped with uniforms bearing the trade name Elco 30; Chief of Police William O'Leary arrested George Bayley for speeding around town while demonstrating the Elco 30 to prospective buyers and an Elco 30 completed a record run of 278 miles, from Danville, Illinois to Sidney, in exactly 12 hours, all the while consuming exactly 12 gallons of gasoline. It appeared as if the buying public were becoming acquainted with the name Bimel, but when the first annual Sidney automobile show opened in late April in the two-story-high Miles Garage, located at the corner of Fair Avenue and Walnut Street, the names Hupmobile, Allen, Meteor, Pullman, Sphinx, Buick and Price were conspicuously mentioned in the press. The brand name "Elco" was prominent only in its absence, even though the company had announced testing of the Sidney-based vehicle had been underway for several months. Nevertheless, hopes were high and apparently warranted. By July, four Elco 30s were rolling off the assembly line every day, and by the end of 1915 some 300 vehicles had been manufactured in Sidney and delivered to localities as distant as Cuba. The next year the company made an equal number of vehicles.

On February 16, 1916, the Bimel Buggy Company was reincorporated as the Bimel Automobile Company. Simultaneously, it increased its capital stock to $500,000, ended its history of carriage production that had dated back to 1844 and introduced a new six-cylinder model designed to compete with automobiles costing $1,000 and up. Thomas M. Miller, the former vice-president, was introduced as president of the new enterprise and described as a "clean cut business man of high moral character."

Billed as the Model Six, the new $995, 115-inch wheelbase Bimel touring car was advertised to weigh 2,400 pounds, complete with a large honeycomb radiator, 15-gallon gas tank, Westinghouse starter and lighting system, speedometer and leather seats. Buyers could choose between black or dark green as the color for their new car. Bimel upgraded assembly line operations to make the new model available by April 1, and supposedly achieved this deadline, but within the span of a mere few months the future of the company was in serious doubt. Sales were declining, World War I was enveloping Europe and rumors were circulating that the federal government might soon curtail the manufacture of automobiles. The *Sidney Daily News* succinctly summarized the developing conditions by reporting: "All this means that the man intending to buy a new car in the spring will stand a poor chance of getting delivery."

In December, Mr. Miller took matters into his own hands, and three days after Christmas sold $1,800 of Bimel Automobile Stock to Miss Anna M. Jelley at her home off State Route 47, in Turtle Creek Township, west of Hardin. During his sales pitch, he was reported to have stated the Bimel Company had zero debts and was flourishing, prosperous and making lots of money, but needed even more financial resources for the purchase of additional material. On or about the same time a similar pitch was made to Esther Jelley, Anna's sister, Edward S. McClure and Mrs. P. O. Stockstill, all of whom bought stock on the supposition it was a better investment than any bank or building or loan association.

It was all to no avail. Several months later when the Bimel Automobile Company was placed in the hands of receivers, it had debts of $175,000, balanced against an inventory of assets valued at $50,000. In May 1917, the remaining physical assets, minus the grounds, buildings and 15 completed automobiles, were sold to the American Motor Parts Company of Indianapolis for a mere $15,715. Unnamed parties purchased the cars, four- and six-cylinder roadsters and touring cars, all together valued at $5,120. The Bimel Automobile Company was history but the alleged chicanery of its president had yet to be addressed.

Thomas Milo Miller was arraigned in Common Pleas Court on Saturday, November 3, 1917, charged with making false representations to Anna Jelley. He entered a plea of not guilty. Bond was set at $5,000, and the trial in the case of the State of Ohio vs. T. M. Miller was set to begin the next month.

During his testimony, Mr. Miller vehemently denied all charges and maintained his belief the Bimel Automobile Company was in a prosperous condition up to the time it went into the hands of the receivers, even though he had begun to sell his stock in November of 1916. When it was revealed other executives of the company had sold their stock during the same period of time, the tenor of the courtroom changed.

The four-day trial ended in the late afternoon of Thursday, December 20, and several hours later the ten-man jury returned a verdict of guilty as charged. Mr. Miller was sentenced to a three-year prison term, but almost immediately the sentence was altered to parole. The only possible explanation for a decision that riled the community at large was the fact that during the trial ten resolute members of Sidney had testified to the outstanding character of the defendant, a long-term member of the M. E. Methodist Church, where he served as a Sunday School teacher.

Given his freedom, Mr. Miller immediately left town and moved to Indianapolis, where he became involved in the real estate business. With his departure, all hopes that Sidney might become a Detroit-of-the-future were dashed. Considering the fact the Motor City was facing the possibility of bankruptcy in the second decade of the 21st century, perhaps the failure of the Bimel automobile was just as well.

COUTURIER TO THE CELEBRATED

His creations were known by a variety of names: Dolphin, French Poupee, Straw Sailor, Pussy-Willow, Leghorn Straw and Venetian Blind. Examples of his work have been on display in the Metropolitan Museum of Art, while others are safely tucked away in private collections. He expounded on "Color and Its Effect on Our Lives" to audiences of the Columbia Broadcasting System and shared his ideas on feminine fashion over the airwaves of the National Broadcasting Company. Caught in a whim of audacity, he once suggested men would be more comfortable if they "twirled a fan when the weather is hot." Subscribers to *Harpers Bazaar* gained exclusive insight into his monthly suggestions on interior decoration and designs of quaint costumes. Glitterati of stage, screen and Fifth Avenue -- Billie Burke, Mrs. A. F. Tiffany, Florenz Ziegfeld, Mary Pickford, Irene Castle, Mrs. Waldorf Astor and Mrs. C. Dana Gibson -- demanded he "dress them" in ensembles of originality and exclusivity. Sensitive to the public's opinion of male couturiers, he remembered a past as a "former football star" who regularly engaged in tennis competitions and boxing exercises delivered "with a sledge hammer punch," even as the press occasionally recalled him as a "temperamental boy given to dressing his sister's dolls." His work was most favorably compared to that of Paul Poiret, the French fashion designer whose contributions to 20th century fashion have been likened to Picasso's contributions to 20th century art. To grande dames, dowagers and assorted members of "The Smart Set," he was the Ralph Lauren of the 1910s, 1920s and the 1930s.

When he cautioned should "you match your hair by night and your eyes by day you will never be amiss," the women of America raced to be the first in line at the local beauty saloon.

Herman Patrick Tappe was born on Tuesday, June 20, 1876, in Sidney, Ohio, the only son of Herman F. and Anna Tappe. A member of a Cincinnati family that manufactured musical instruments, Herman Sr., moved to Sidney and opened a store northeast of the public square where he sold his personal brand of cigars, made in the family factory located at the southern end of Ohio Avenue. While cigar-making was the focus of his livelihood, music was the foundation of his extracurricular interests, and in 1874 he rounded up a group of similarly inspired young men and formed the "Tappe Silver Star Cornet Band." Quickly melding into a coordinated and popular assemble, the Tappe band became the feature event of many a public program, including the occasions of the laying of the cornerstone of both the Monumental Building and the Court House. With his reputation as a bandmaster still on the ascent, "Professor" Tappe was stricken with tuberculosis in 1883. Accompanying his body as it was being taken to Graceland Cemetery, the Tappe band played funereal music in a manner described by the local press as "New Orleans style."

Anna Tappe was born in Ireland during the first year of the infamous "potato famine" and came to the United States with her family at the age of three. Left a widow with four children, Herman, Jr. and three daughters, Mayme, Celia and Elizabeth, she lived the rest of her life quietly in Sidney. She never remarried and died in 1937, at the age of 92.

Herman Jr., graduated from Holy Angels High School, a member of the fifth class to earn a comprehensive 12-year curriculum diploma, and began his career working in the millinery department of the Thedieck department store. There he learned the rudiments of the women's clothing business and made many a mental note as Ignatius Thedieck periodically made business trips to New York and Paris, returning with fashions of a quality such that "Sidney ladies always had the latest fashions from which to choose."

With his learning curve leveling out, Herman left Sidney and joined the staff of John T. Shayne & Company, a Chicago Loop-based women's clothier widely lauded as "the largest business of its kind outside of New York City." Having opened the doors to his emporium in 1884, John T. worked diligently to establish a reputation as a civic leader, Democratic politician and an importer and distribution agent of fine furs. His position in business and society was secured when the New York Times reported the number of awards he received for exhibits displayed at the 1893 World's Fair left "no doubt that the Shayne fur products surpass those made in any part of the world." Herman's knowledge of the couturier trade had taken another big step forward.

Moving to New York City in the pivotal year of 1900, he signed on with Wurzberger and Hecht, wholesale dealers in flowers and feathers, clothing accessories then considered "haute couture" by leading ladies everywhere. Hired specifically as a foreign buyer, Herman began an extended series of often semi-annual Atlantic crossings to Paris and other European style centers, always traveling in comfort on such illustrious ocean liners as the *Baltic, Mauretania* and *Aquitania*.

Afflicted by an "endless quest for the beautiful in life," Herman would occasionally find himself in embarrassing positions during these travels. Leaving England in 1916, he was held by customs authorities who questioned a shipment of "the cutest little assortment...of Scotch kilts (adorned) with their wee sporrans...they had ever laid eyes on." Suspecting he was "getting ready to equip Scotch-Irish rebels down Dublin way," they "dragged him from the Ritz in London to the Vine Street jail." Only after Lady Paget, diarist, writer and intimate friend of Queen Victoria, vouched for his reputation and Herman explained the costumes were meant to "grace the forms of fair American women on the golf links" was he released.

During another crossing "a famous pianist whose name is Taxi---something" made mention of the beauty of a fellow passenger. Herman's inherent love for the beautiful led him to the woman's boudoir. History does not record what transpired there, but later he vehemently "denied that he sat on her bed and kissed her." As the *Piqua Daily Press* summarized "Herman…gets a whole lot more publicity gratis than he is entitled to."

On his way home from a buying trip in 1906, Herman made the acquaintance of Mrs. Ada Jaffray McVickar, a willowy, six-foot-tall widow graced with carriage and snow-white hair. Undaunted by the 25 years that separated their ages and encouraged by the ostensible depth of resources that supported her independent lifestyle, he was smitten, she was enthralled and a romance born on the high seas blossomed into marriage a year later on May 20, on the alter of St. Leo's Church, New York City, the Reverend Father Ducay officiating. Born in 1851, Ada was the daughter of Edward Somerville Jaffray, senior partner in a prominent mercantile firm, member of the Union League and the Yacht Club, and for half a century one of the most successful of New York's business men.

In the true spirit of an unconventional wedding, one of Herman's sisters acted as the maid of honor to the bride, while James, one of five sons Ada brought to the union, functioned as best man to the six-foot-three-inch tall groom. A small reception was held in "The Wyoming," an elegant, sprawling, French Renaissance-style apartment building that Ada called her home when she was not residing in her country estate, "Ardsley-on-Hudson." The very next day the happy couple set sail for a summer-long tour of Europe.

Once they had returned home, Ada financed Herman in his first venture as a "man-milliner" at 4 West 40th Street and induced J. Pierpont Morgan, the noted financier, to add a few of his millions of dollars to the operating budget. Initially the partnership thrived, largely due to the fact it "attracted many of the society people in Mrs. Tappe's set," but by September of 1911 company cash flow had reached a new low and a petition for bankruptcy was filed, the result of "the number of accounts left unpaid by society folk." It was another game-changing event in Herman's life, since ten months earlier he had received a divorce from Ada after having been "separated and reunited several times." Ada died in September 1917 and took to her grave the answer to the question: Did she ever receive the $2,000 in yearly alimony Herman promised?

In the years leading up to America's entry into World War I, Herman was involved in a whirlwind of activities. Discarding the 155 creditors to his bankruptcy and fueled by enthusiasm and hope, he somehow found the resources to open a new shop, the House of Tappe Inc., at 25 West 57th Street. Several years later, during one of his periodic trips to Sidney, he announced he would spare no expense in building his mother a beautiful home on the site once occupied by the family cigar factory.

When completed "The Chimneys" became the source of immense pride for Herman, as evidenced by the wording in a note written decades later by my father, Lionel A. Dickas: "I was a delivery boy for Thedieck's Dept store -- delivered a package -- Herman Tappe gave me a $2.00 tip and showed me through the Chimneys--I was 13." This event took place in 1915, mere months after construction was completed, and is suggestive of the depth of Herman's generosity of time and money. That long ago tip would today have the value of $47.00.

An innovation of the 57th Street store was the presence of models, employed to give bodily presence and feminine allure to Herman's creations. One of the first to interview, a slim, regal, sweet, 16-year old girl who gave her name as Anna Holch and admitted she had no working experience whatsoever, was hired without further ado. Months later, disturbed by the loss of a star "mannequin" -- then a popular term for a fashion model, -- Herman noticed for the first time, reflected in one of the store's mirrors, the fine profile of "Miss Anna." Over the ensuing years business and romance played at odds, but around the time the Armistice was signed the couple had agreed to marriage. The wedding took place in St. Patrick's Cathedral on December 19, 1918, a magical event between a groom now known around Manhattan as the "Fifth Avenue Adonis" and a bride considered far and wide as "the most beautiful model in America."

In a stellar recognition of both an end to the war and his marriage to Anna, Herman made arrangements to sponsor a Victory Ball in Sidney, with no expense spared. After all, the *Shelby County Democrat* had recently announced his "income for last year is reputed to have been a hundred thousand dollars." Five hundred invitations were mailed, women fought over a diminishing supply of decolleté gowns, the services of the Parker Jazz Band and the Heidelberg Orchestra were engaged and the Armory was decorated in fluttering flags and a thousand yards of patriotically colored bunting. When she arrived, the new Mrs. Herman Tappe, enveloped in a "gown of cloth of silver, enhanced with Madonna velvet," was escorted by footmen beneath a canopy and into the Chinese-lantern-festooned auditorium. The assembled revelers danced and celebrated until 3:30 in the morning of December 31. It was a night the Valley City would not soon forget.

When they returned to their newly purchased home, the couple signed an agreement making them equal partners in the 57th Street establishment, and life went on -- well, at least for awhile. Within 24 months, the bloom was off the rose. While they worked together during the day, at night connubial bliss turned to connubial mayhem as Anna moved into the Ritz and Herman into a cloistered apartment. The tabloids were agog with revelation as they published full-page rotogravure-style reviews. Said she, "Herman, I love you but marriage is getting on my nerves." Said he, "But you said it -- the wedding bells are cracked." Blasé New York City, very much acquainted with sensational separations, sat up and gasped, "just another Tappe sensation."

The Tappes were determined to stay married while living apart, but their relationship deteriorated further. Anna opened a shop of her own in competition with her estranged husband. An irate husband, an ex-pugilist and man-about-the theatrical-district, filed a $100,000 alienation of affection suit against Herman. Herman bounced back by publically naming several prominent "love tycoons" who had been seen in Anna's loving embrace.

Through it all Herman remained undeterred and improved on his reputation against all odds. Traveling to Hollywood, he designed the costumes for the 1921 French Revolution thriller, "Orphans of the Storm," staring Lillian and Dorothy Gish. Along Broadway he was given costume design credit for the plays "Uncle Vanya," "Polly With a Past" and "Go Easy Mabel." Knowing publicity was essential to business longevity, he caused society to choke when he declared the color white would be banished from his wedding gowns -- "shell pink is best." That same society cooed when he announced, "I expect the cape to prove the first choice of the smart woman."

By 1930 he was working out of a new address, 9 West 57th Street, where he sewed his new label, "Tappe Modes" to his inventory of sables, ermines and rare brocades. That year he traveled home, bringing with him gowns of his design for the bride and her attendants at the Weis-Thedieck wedding at Holy Angels Church. Four years later he moved his emporium to 12 West 40th Street, under the sponsorship of "DoDo" Dorrance the millionaire Campbell soup heiress. Time was running out on Herman, however, and as war clouds gathered again he was reduced to extolling the merits of the dashboard of the 1936 Dodge in a national advertisement.

Herman Patrick Tappe died on Monday, September 20, 1954, at the age of 78. By today's standards of dress, ruled by the T-shirt, torn jeans and flip-flops, his style of apparel would be labeled archaic, irrelevant and possibly even extinct. But during that four-decade period when fashion reigned supreme and "haute couture" influenced those persons who set the tone for society he was "that quaint, original genius," the "master of New York's mecca of modes," the "milliner to the 400" --- the Couturier to the Celebrated.

Major Edward Bowes and his famous gong.

MOMENTS OF FAME

In the very early years, those during which it was clawing its way out of the frontier, Sidney was a community generally lacking in culture. Perhaps the stagecoach brought the occasional juggler or Shakespearean orator to town, but those now-and-then events were conducted without advance publicity, the audiences were sparse and often ill-of-understanding and the performers were quickly forgotten.

Beyond the confines of the Valley City, however, the world of entertainment was growing, both in diversity and innovation. In 1885, partners Benjamin Keith and Edward Albee developed the classic theatrical format that was quickly dubbed "vaudeville," a designation named after the Val de Vire sector of the Province of Normandy in France, a region known for its extensive repertoire of folk ballads.

The very first American "vaudeville saloon" curtain was raised in 1840 in Boston, and soon this new form of show business began to supersede traveling minstrel shows, the public appeal of which peaked immediately following the years of the Civil War. By 1896, New York City was home to seven vaudeville houses and Chicago boasted an even half-a-dozen. The era of the "song and dance man," the mime, stunt cyclist, buffoon comedian and warbling soprano was born.

Not until the dawn of the 20th century, however, did Sidney become part of a vaudeville circuit, an organized chain of theatres between which acts traveled back and forth. With Ms. Blanch Young seated in the box office and Ms. Bertha Rebstock positioned at the piano, the curtain rose at 7:30 on the evening of December 10, 1906, marking the grand opening of the Orpheum Theatre at 115 South Ohio Avenue. An era of "polite vaudeville catering to ladies and children" was inaugurated in Sidney, and its' citizens showered accolades on Mary Mannering as she concluded her weeklong portrayal of "Glorious Betsy."

With reports of "hundreds turned away" and left "outside trying to get in," this widely talked-about extravaganza spelled the beginning of organized and continuing entertainment in Sidney. Within a decade, the cluster of four vaudeville theatres occupying the east side of the 100 block of North Main Street gave show business definition to Sidney's "Great White Way," the local equivalent of the 42nd Street theatrical district of New York City.

The changing advertising format of the Mall Theatre, owned and operated by Bertram Binkley, a native-son of Sidney, was typical of this handful of entertainment emporiums. Following a period of extensive remodeling in 1914 that included the installation of a "sanitary drinking fountain," the coming-attraction placards displayed outside the box office introduced programming that was undergoing change from "vaudeville only" to "vaudeville with movies." The focus of the American entertainment industry was shifting from 42nd Street first to Hollywood, and then with the advent of radio to all points north, east, south and west.

When KDKA in Pittsburgh, Pennsylvania, went on the air on November 2, 1920, broadcasting the results of the presidential elections, the history of show business in America changed forever. As the first licensed commercial station, it gave the entertainment-seeking public a choice: an expensive evening at the theatre dressed in top-hat, tails and evening clothes or a free stay at home warmly wrapped in a night gown, pajamas and robe, listening to the radio.

By the end of 1921, four well-financed stations effectively linked New York City with Boston, Chicago and Pittsburgh, and a growing sense of excitement arose as broadcasting activities became more organized. In December, two American Telephone and Telegraph engineers wrote a memorandum outlining steps necessary for the establishment of a national radio network. Five years later, the National Broadcasting Company was formed, to be joined soon thereafter by the Columbia Broadcasting System and the Mutual Broadcasting System.

During the early years, programming was mostly commercial-free and entertainers performed "gratis," hoping ultimately to become financially involved in this revolutionary innovation. Eventually, advertising-supported private stations became the standard for the American broadcasting networks, and wireless operations supporting the local community sprang up across the length and breadth of the country, but not without a few difficulties.

Radio without programming was like a voice lacking a holler and what was this new medium meant to deliver? Would it be a constant stream of farm livestock and egg prices, the "bid and ask" of Wall Street transactions, an exchange of kitchen recipes or the reporting of ever-changing weather conditions? Station repertoires early-on varied in response to listener needs, but soon the airwaves reached ever further over the landscape, delivering programs designed around individuals who could entertain not so much with "You-need-to-hear," as with "You-wish-to-hear" content.

One of the first of this newly launched talent of nationally known radio personalities was a rectangular-faced, imperious individual who insisted upon being addressed as "Major," a title associated with either active duty during World War I or service in the post-war Officer Reserve Corps.

Born in San Francisco on June 14, 1874, Edward Bowes' carefree childhood years were cut short at the age of six when his father died. Any concept of a continuing education ended when he left grammar school and began demonstrating a keen sense of business acumen, starting as an office boy and then advancing into the world of real estate. Left penniless after the cataclysmic earthquake of 1906, he moved east in search of new opportunities. With a flair for music, he readily found employment in New York City as a conductor, composer and arranger and successfully used these talents in the production of several Broadway stage productions, notably "Kindling" in 1911 and "The Bridal Path" two years later.

Expanding his hopes and aspirations ever further, Bowes became the driving force behind the construction of the Capitol Theatre, an imposing movie palace located at 1645 Broadway, directly across the avenue from the famous Winter Garden Theatre. Designed by Thomas W. Lamb, the Capitol opened its doors on October 24, 1919, and was quickly filled to capacity with a standing room only crowd of 4,000 first night revelers. With Bowes as managing director and a marquee slogan of "The Worlds Largest Theatre," the Capitol soon became one of the first of the large, lavish movie theatres that were to dominate the film industry for the next four decades.

Never content with the status quo, the Major in 1926 launched, as yet another promotional device, an amateur night stage presentation titled "Major Bowes and His Capitol Family." The Roaring Twenties were under way, and America was undergoing a decade-long extravaganza defined by excessive attitudes and lifestyles. Competitive, amateur presentations were a form of entertainment well designed for the tenure of the times.

Moving to radio station WHN in April of 1934, Bowes gained even greater success with his show, now renamed "The Original Amateur Hour." Two years later the weekly, hour-long program was reaching out to a national audience through stations controlled by the Columbia Broadcasting System. The rest is radio history.

Each week Bowes would engage in a friendly form of banter with the contestants and then listen, often somewhat impatiently, to their performances. A wide range of performers -- tap dancers, jugglers, musicians, baton twirlers and singers -- took the stage and did their best until the Major more often than not intoned "All right, all right," rang a large gong and sent the unfortunate participant home. The listening public loved it, and soon Bowes's managerial savvy had forged the radio show into several profitable touring units that visited theatres in cities both large and small across America.

PASSAGES

Major Bowes and his chief talent scout Ted Mack auditioned more than a million wannabe entertainment stars throughout the 36-year-long span of "The Original Amateur Hour." Only an estimated one-half of one percent became professional, but that small circle of winners included such well-known performers as comedians Jack Carter and Alan King, opera singers Beverly Sills, Lily Pons and Robert Merrill and pop singers Teresa Brewer, Pat Boone and Frank Sinatra. Lesser-known show business personalities included the Swiss bell ringer Harvey Mearns, Duane Sister the acrobatic dancer, Neva Ames the xylophone wonder and, of great significance to radio listeners in the Shelby County area, Whistling Joe and His Buddies.

By the time the trio of Kenny Ringlespaugh, Stanley Harper and Joseph Gutman had graduated from Sidney High School in the early 1930s, they were already well known around Sidney. Their signature act consisted of a mixture of singing and dancing, supported by Stan on violin, Kenny on his guitar and Joe, the front man, pursing his lips into a whistling version of "Listen to the Mockingbird."

After they had won an amateur night contest on the stage of the Ohio Theatre, they received an invitation to audition for the New York City-based "Amateur Hour." Proof that they had succeeded in that initial test was contained in a strangely worded telegram sent to Sidney Mayor Rolla Laughlin on the first of November, 1935: "Will be on Major Bowes program this coming Sunday, November third. Whistling Joe and His Buddies."

Supposedly everyone with access to a radio in Sidney the following Sunday evening had his or her ear glued to the airwaves as the trio made their appearance toward the end of the hour-long program. During the introduction, Joe said he was employed in a coal yard, while one of his buddies worked as a paperhanger, the other as a machinist. The Major then launched into a typical monologue during which he bragged about his show visiting small-town America, giving national attention to the wondrous qualities and enhancing environments found there.

Fred Allen, the emcee of perhaps the best and most sophisticated radio show of its era, once lampooned Bowes' speaking style in words both humorous and caustic:

Tonight we salute that quaint old city nested back in those peaceful hills. . .the city we all love and venerate: two hundred miles of hail-fellow-well-met. Here the first eyedropper was made. Here it was that John Brundle jumped out of a window, landed on his rubber heels, and got the idea for the first pogo stick. . .the first hot-dog stand not to charge for its mustard was opened here. Tonight we salute . . .tonight. . .tonight our honor city is . . . .

For the record, the *Sidney Daily News* published the actual introduction. When asked where Sidney was located, Joe replied, "about 40 miles north of Dayton, 95 miles north of Cincinnati." In answer to the Major's next question, "What place is to the north of it?" Joe replied, "It's 70 miles west of Columbus." Somewhat exasperated, the Major finally introduced the trio as arriving "from Sidney, some where north of the equator."

One week later the results were announced; Whistling Joe and His Buddies had placed fourth in the competition, good enough to be given the opportunity to appear with one of the national tour groups sponsored by the "Amateur Hour." The arrival of a second telegram, however, gave their budding career even greater clarity: "Major Bowes wants you in New York on Sunday, November 17th. Important."

Arriving in New York City, the trio learned they had been chosen to be part of the program of Unit Number 10, scheduled to begin, on the first of December, a year-long tour that opened on the east coast and closed in California, with the Ohio Theatre one of the stops on its itinerary.

The day Unit 10 came to town, Thursday, January 9, 1936, had already been designated "Major Bowes Day." The grand celebration started off with presentation of the keys to the city and an appreciation dinner given at the Wagner House, sponsored by the Sidney Merchants Association and the Sidney Chamber of Commerce. More than one hundred "interested citizens" attended the "seventy-five cents per plate" luncheon.

The ceremonies then moved to the stage of the Warner Ohio Theatre where "continuous showings until midnight" began promptly at 2:30 PM. The theatre was reportedly packed with a standing room only audience from "the opening until the close." The highlight of the entire day occurred, however, during the first show of the evening when the hometown trio appeared on stage. Immediately prior to their appearance, E. C. Amos, president of the Merchants Association, gleefully confirmed the rumor that had been floating around town by announcing he had indeed sent Bowes a telegram stating: "Congratulations on locating Sidney more definitely than just somewhere north of the equator."

Major Edward Bowes died in 1946, on the eve of his 72nd birthday, at his Rumson, New Jersey home. Ted Mack stepped into the Amateur Hour emcee position and two years later guided the program into the emerging field of television. The show was lauded as one of the longest running of show-biz entertainments when its final program was televised in 1970 over the facilities of the Columbia Broadcasting System. Its audience had finally begun to decline, but it is reported some 10 million, faithful-to-the-end viewers sat before their television sets during the last show hoping some aspiring amateur might be launched to fame and fortune.

The Capitol Theatre became the favored site for film premieres in New York City and remained such for decades, starting with "The Wizard of Oz" in 1939 and continuing to the grand opening of the 2 hour, 19 minute long epic "2001: A Space Odyssey," on January 1, 1968. Nine months later, the curtain fell for the last time on the stage of the Capitol, heralded for its' nearly half century of entertainment history by an all-star benefit featuring Bob Hope and an up-and-coming talent, Johnny Carson. The venerable Times Square landmark was quickly demolished and replaced by the 48-story high Paramount Plaza office tower.

Joe Gutman and his buddies are now part of the past, their story but a footnote in the annals of American entertainment history. For one brief shining moment, however, their show-business star -- kept in radiant condition by Major Bowes -- truly lit up the skies over Shelby County. In looking back to that distant time, it seems only appropriate to recall, in memory of Joe and Stan and Kenny, the words Bob Hope famously used when closing each of his radio shows -- "Thanks for the Memories."

EPISODES OF EMANCIPATION

The message, written by the poet Emma Lazarus and displayed beneath the Statue of Liberty, officially named "Liberty Enlightening the World," says it all:

> Give me your tired, your poor,
> Your huddled masses, yearning to breathe free,
> The wretched refuse of your teeming masses,
> Send these, the homeless tempest-tost to me,
> I lift my lamp beside the golden door.

Dedicated to the millions of immigrants who arrived in the New World from their respective "old worlds," the poem has also given hope to the millions of Americans who through the result of birth or circumstance have found themselves yearning or fighting for emancipation: the process of being set free from legal, social or political restrictions.

America was conceived on a foundation of emancipation, but the promise has not always become the product. The native born were denied freedom in treaties signed and broken in the rush to manifest destiny. Those brought ashore in shackles were told they didn't deserve freedom and most lived a life of slavery. Many a young man's future was placed on hold while he went to a war fought, at home or abroad, for the declared purpose of emancipating a population caught in the grip of any number of social systems deemed worse than death.

Shelby County has paid its dues for seeking freedom for various groups of humanity. It once acted as a home, and way station, to those escaping the wrongs of racial discrimination. It has supplied the mind and muscle for multiple wars. The episodes cover more than a century of history and are both melancholy and inspirational.

RANDOLPH'S BUCKEYE LEGACY

The history of slavery in North America begins with the voyages of Ponce de Leon, the Spanish conquistador who in 1513 discovered Florida while supposedly in the process of searching for the Fountain of Youth. His shipboard crew included individuals of African descent, freemen who signed on to conduct any odd job that needed to be done, offshore or onshore. When this population of volunteers was depleted, there followed an era of conscription that will forever blot the history of New World exploration: persons were drafted against their will and transported across the Atlantic Ocean in chains. Between the year 1500 and the first decade of the 19th century some 12 million Africans were forced to leave their tribal homes and travel to the new lands of the west. It is estimated some 10 million completed the voyages. The rest were buried at sea, the victims of malnutrition and unbelievably difficult on-board conditions in sweltering cargo rooms.

Slavery in colonial America had a slow start. By 1750, the slave population of the 13 original colonies was slightly less than 240,000, some 20 percent of the total population of 1,171,000. The majority of the slaves -- a full 86 percent -- were scattered throughout the states of Georgia, Maryland, North and South Carolina and Virginia. Virginia was, by and large, the home base for the greatest number of American slaves, adding up to almost a half a million by the onset of the Civil War.

As plantation-based agriculture spread outward from Jamestown and up the valleys of the James, York, Rappahannock and Potomac Rivers, the demand for field workers exceeded the number of colonial residents and persons in England willing to do such laborious work. During the 1660s the colony of Virginia revised its laws such that Blacks could be maintained in a state of perpetual servitude on a permanent basis, year after year after year. The result was an influx of slaves, imported both through the Caribbean islands and directly from Africa and employed primarily in the planting and harvesting of the labor-intensive crops of tobacco and cotton.

On the eve of the Civil War, the great majority of the slave population of Virginia lived in counties located to the southeast of the Blue Ridge Mountains. There, plantations established on the relatively flat lands of the Piedmont physiographic province supported slave populations commonly numbering 50 and more persons, with a few holding more than 500 slaves. In contrast, counties within the Shenandoah Valley and those of the Valley and Ridge Province of the Appalachian Mountains that constituted territory that would eventually be separated as the State of West Virginia had far fewer slaves, on average fifteen or less.

Charlotte County is typical of those counties that together formed the slave belt of Virginia. The economy of this 477-square-mile landscape of subdued, rolling hills has, since colonial times, been solely dependent on agriculture. Even today, its rural atmosphere is defined not only by fewer than 13,000 residents, but also by the fact it is one of only three counties in Virginia that do not contain a single traffic signal. At one time, however, during its glory years, it was lauded as the home of two notables: Patrick Henry, the "give me liberty, or give me death" patriot who lent his signature to the United States Declaration of Independence; and John Randolph, the owner of 8,000 acres of prime Roanoke River bottomlands who left a legacy of history that extended as far north as the environs of Shelby County, Ohio.

In his lifetime John Randolph wore many hats: a long-time member of both the U. S. House of Representatives and the U. S. Senate, the designated 8th U. S. Minister to Russia and as "John Randolph of Roanoke," a moniker that separated him from his father of the same name. Born June 2, 1773, in Prince Georges County, Virginia, to John Randolph, a prosperous tobacco farmer, and his wife Frances Bland, he is reputed to have been a descendent of the Native-American princess Pocahontas, daughter of Powhatan, chief of the Tsenacommacah confederacy of tribal groups and wife of John Rolfe, a farmer credited with the first cultivation of tobacco as an export crop in the Colony of Virginia. While still a young man, he contracted tuberculosis, the effects of which left him beardless and speaking with a high-pitched voice. Following a disjointed series of studies conducted at the College of New Jersey, Princeton and Columbia, he studied the law in Philadelphia.

At the ripe-young age of 26, Randolph was elected to the U. S. House of Representatives, where he quickly gained a reputation as an astute and popular speaker, a flashy dresser and as an eccentric striding about the nations capital with a whip in hand, in imitation, it was whispered, of members of the British Parliament. For the next quarter of a century, he fought against what he considered "creeping nationalism," differed now and then with his cousin, President Thomas Jefferson, made clear his opposition to the War of 1812 and, in general, advocated a system of political stability with minimal governmental interference. Elevated to the U. S. Senate in 1825, he fathered the very first Senate filibuster by speaking for several days in opposition to a measure proposed by President John Quincy Adams. Following a stint as Minister to Russia, he again served in Congress until his death in 1833. He died a bachelor, having lived a life marked by a trait of religious piety.

Randolph's bellicose personality was complicated by bouts of heavy drinking and the infrequent use of opium, aids employed to combat pain associated with his extended battle with tuberculosis. Throughout it all he maintained common cause with those closely associated to him, especially the slaves he housed on his plantation. Opposed in theory to slavery, but aware of its economic value to antebellum Virginia, he left a will that not only contained a codicil stipulating the emancipation of the Randolph slaves, but also provided money for their settlement on land to be purchased in the "free state of Ohio." Though his brother contested the will on the basis of supposed insanity, it was finally upheld as legal and abiding.

On June 10, 1846, 13 years after gaining status as free persons, 383 Randolph slaves packed their meager belongings into 16 horse-drawn wagons and began an arduous trip north and northwest to their promised land, guided by a wagon master who was familiar with the projected route. Ages varied from that of a babe-in-arms to "Granny Hannah," rumored to be over a century old. Their passage was tortuous and long, so much so they feared they would never reach their destination. Amenities along the trail were few and far between. Like their white counterparts then seeking new lands at the end of the Oregon Trail, some walked and others rode between campsites set up along the trailside at days' end.

With the assembly of horses, wagons, people and wagon master completed the caravan bid farewell to the Piedmont bottomlands of the Randolph Plantation and headed northwest across the forested peaks of the Blue Ridge Mountains and into the grassy vistas of the Shenandoah Valley. With the northeastern extensions of Brush Mountain and the ramparts of Peters Mountain at their back, the view ahead swept across the verdant valley of the Greenbrier River. There, in the small community of Lewisburg, the lead wagon rolled onto the right-of-way of the James River and Kanawha Turnpike, the ancient buffalo and Indian trail across the Sewell Mountain Range that was upgraded in 1824 and today is designated as U. S. Route 60. Circumventing the challenging relief of the New River Valley and bypassing the 15-foot-drop of the Kanawha Falls, the travelers continued along the east bank of the Kanawha River and arrived at Charlestown on June 16. There they sought passage on a river steamer to the Ohio River port of Cincinnati. On July 1, they traipsed down the center of Main Street in a manner the *Cincinnati Daily Chronicle* described as not unlike a "drive of sheep coming to market." Reaching the dockside of the Miami and Erie Canal, they purchased passage for the 100-mile trip north by barge to Mercer County, their promised new home.

Their entry into the State of Ohio was anticipated with a sense of final delivery and freedom, for carefully hidden within the accumulation of their worldly goods was a certificate signed by the Clerk of Court of Charlotte County, Virginia, attesting to their freedom--- "a true list and description of the Negroes and mulattoes emancipated by the will of John Randolph of Roanoke, dec'd, recorded in the General Court of Virginia, made out from the general book of registers of free Negroes and mulattoes... approved by the said court the 4th day of May 1846."

Unfortunately, these words, however recorded and protected by law, did not ensure an easy and uneventful trip upriver through the Great Miami River Valley. They met resistance in Tipp City and Troy and then Piqua, where the town marshal denied them a much-desired quaff of water, claiming a local shortage of this readily available resource. In general, their arrival at many points was accompanied by the retort: "Just keep on moving up the canal!"

Continuing north, the close-knit band of travelers crossed into Shelby County, maneuvered through the locks at Locksport (now Lockington), bypassed Sidney and moved on to Berlin (now Fort Loramie), where they were not allowed to stretch their legs on shore, even for a brief moment. *The Sidney Journal* later recounted the arrival of the Randolph group in Berlin as being met by a "mob (that) received them with sticks and stones," a reception that reportedly caused one of the slaves to surmise: "his Master (that being John Randolph) was his best friend, after all." More apprehensive than optimistic, the group again cast off to the north.

When they reached the wharf at Bremen (present-day New Bremen), now only a few miles from the land promised them through the will of John Randolph, they were met by a large crowd of residents. After allowing them to decamp for the evening, the residents went into discussions regarding the theme "What do we do now?" Reaching a consensus, they returned to the temporary Randolph camp and in an environment fraught with tension proclaimed their decision:

> We will not live among the Negroes, as we have settled here first, we have fully determined that we will resist the settlement of blacks and mulattoes in the county to the full extent of our means, the bayonet not excepted.

The Miami and Erie Canal barge master, a man by the name of Cardwell, was then forced to charter two canal boats to be used to transport the entire Randolph troop back down the canal -- out of Mercer County. An escort of armed settlers accompanied them.

Broken-hearted, scared and bewildered after having endured years of slavery, more than a dozen years of legal debate, a difficult passage over the Appalachian Mountains and up the Great Miami River, the Randolph group began to break into separate populations. A few of them allegedly walked 9 miles west to the community of Carthagena, a colony of predominantly free Blacks founded in 1835 by Augustus Wattles, a Quaker teacher from Connecticut who dreamed of opening a school for African Americans in the vicinity. Unfortunately, their arrival there was not unlike that at Bremen, as they were met by a tawdry mob of whites, additional evidence of the scattered degree of racial prejudice that existed in Ohio before the Civil War.

Others added to the population count of the small community of Rumley, a Shelby County crossroads village located along the old stagecoach route linking Piqua with Lima. Platted in 1837 by Joel and Wesley Goings, this mixed race community prospered until the 1860s when its inhabitants began to scatter elsewhere, encouraged by the wording of posted signs that warned of physical harm if the Black residents did not move to other locations. Today, a handful of structures located near the junction of Blanke Road and Hardin-Wapakoneta Road is the sole remaining homestead evidence of this group of former Virginia slaves described by Henry Howe, in his *History of Ohio*, as "equal to the whites in morals, religion and intelligence."

Some Randolph members, reported to have been as many as a third of the original group, settled in and around Sidney. By some records, certain individuals living in town were perhaps the most open hearted of all the residents of the upper Miami River Valley. Following a meeting of community leaders, led by Guy Kelsey, a wholesale liquor distributor and grocer, and Joseph Cummins, a onetime Clinton township trustee, and reminiscent of the meeting held in Bremen but with a different outcome, it was decided some of the rejected travelers could stay in private homes within the Valley City, with others distributed among families living in nearby farms.

A search of old newspaper accounts gives identity to a few of these individuals: "Old Quasha," who, at the age of 90, could still remember being head wagoner on John Randolph's Virginia plantation; Robert Shelby, the driver of a team of horses in the War of 1812 and the oldest inhabitant of Shelby County when he died in 1885; and Charles Dickerson who came to Sidney at the age of 16 and dropped dead 42 years later while moving his cart along Main Street in front of Shaffer and Albers' grocery. Shadrach White, commonly known as "Buddie Shang," was perhaps the most famous of all Sidney-based Randolph slaves. Described by *The Sidney Journal* as "a peaceable vagrant... who lived by hunting and fishing (and) got his clothes for nothing and his whisky by gathering mint for saloons," he was tried and acquitted by an all-white jury for the 1889 murder of a white, Civil War veteran who lived in Lacyburg, a squalid Fourth Ward shantytown community located south of Water Street.

A sizeable contingent of the Randolph group settled in and around the village of Rossville, a residential area long ago annexed to Piqua. An 1850 census lists 74 Randolph blacks living there in conditions very similar to that of their white neighbors. Riley Sampson, Guy Howell, Gabriel White and Shadrack White (supposedly not the same as Shadrach White of Sidney), all classed as laborers, together owned property worth a declared $950, an impressive sum when compared to the $1,100 worth of property owned by white members of the same community. The history of Rossville can be surmised by the names and words inscribed on the 134 graves located in the African-Jackson Cemetery tucked away in a sparsely populated wooded area on Zimmerlin Road, on the northern edge of Piqua.

The last group of wandering Randolph slaves were absorbed by the villages of Hanktown, near West Milton and Marshalltown, near Troy. Their dream of community cohesiveness shattered once and for all, the band of Randolph slaves had now became scattered throughout western Ohio

The Randolph Ex-Slaves Association was organized on Thursday, July 24, 1902, at Midway Park, near Piqua. In attendance at the inaugural meeting were 62 members of the original group, born in Virginia, held in slavery and then brought to Ohio as young adults and children. They were immediately recognized as "Old Dominions," a distinction that separated them from the "Buckeyes," those family members who had been born in Ohio or who were children of the original settlers. Throughout the years, reunions were held in Piqua, Troy and the Shelby County fairgrounds, with attendances ranging from 100 to 300. At the 1904 gathering, Isham Randolph, the first male child born after the freed slaves had arrived in Ohio, delivered the greeting to the assembly.

The registration list of the 1905 meeting, held at the Sidney fairgrounds, contained the names of 43 of the original Randolph slaves still living of the 383 that originally traveled overland to Ohio. Of those, 12 were 75 years of age or older.

Written in words that clearly define multiple incidents of confusion, disappointment and unjust decisions, the story of the Randolph slaves is a lengthy one. The details have been well researched and documented and tell a tale of resilience, understanding, patience, fortitude and ultimate acceptance that is scattered over the terrain of three states, hundreds of miles, dozens of years and a handful of generations.

A succinct, terse and melancholy version of the Randolph slave narrative can be found in a back corner of the Rossville cemetery. There, a cluster of headstones identify the grave sites of Louis Musco, Lott Green, George R. Rial, Ed Grouder and Thompson Rial. Each monument bears the name of a Randolph slave, followed by a simple inscription:

BORN A SLAVE
DIED FREE

ESCAPES FROM OPPRESSION

At first glance the sequence of events do seem a bit confusing, but after a few moments of reflection they begin to coalesce into a study of serious intent and righteous endeavor. The topic of statehood for the region the Iroquois called "ohi-yo," meaning "great-river," occupied the premier position on the docket and the debate involved a multi-stage process of review and approval.

Important steps had already been completed. The Northwest Ordinance of 1787 specified the manner in which the various sections of the Northwest Territory would become states. Then, as soon as 5,000 "free men" called the Territory home, a legislature could be formed. The final phase, initiated when 60,000 individuals had taken up residence in a territory, was consideration for statehood.

Thirty-five delegates gathered on Monday, November 1, 1802, in Chillicothe to draft a state constitution. Three months later, on February 19, 1803, Congress recognized its adoption by the elected delegates and declared Ohio the 17th state of the United States of America. Acknowledged as one of the most democratic of legal documents in America, the newly approved constitution contained an article that immediately identified the Buckeye State as a region empowered with liberty -- it prohibited slavery.

The forested landscape of Ohio began to fill quickly with immigrants, many of whom had a strong belief in the concept of emancipation. The more resourceful and determined of these abolitionists established a variety of printed media that advocated an anti-slavery environment. "Dialogue on Slavery," established by James Gilliland in 1820 and "Genius of Universal Emancipation," published around 1821 by Benjamin Lundy were typical examples. The publication date of one of the earliest of these enterprises, "The Philanthropist," established in 1817 in Mt. Pleasant, coincided with the initiation of another undertaking that added to Ohio's reputation as a state conceived with a desire for freedom -- the opening of the Underground Railroad (UR).

Neither a railroad nor generally located beneath the surface of the land, the Underground Railroad was a shadowy system of escape routes and hiding places used from 1816 to 1865 by indentured fugitives seeking safety after they had fled the shackles of the southern slave states and were making their way north to freedom. Blessed with a system of longitudinally oriented rivers and canal routes, a favorable geographical location and the presence of numerous abolitionist and anti-slavery religious groups, Ohio of all the northern states played the most active role in the success of this spider-web plot of trails, corncribs, barns, thickets, basement roosts, attic cubbies and concealed rooms.

In a letter addressed to Professor Wilbur H. Siebert of The Ohio State University, Colonel Dresden Winfield Huston Howard, a 77-year-old, near life-long pioneer of the Maumee River Valley, identified the western reaches of the state as conceivably the oldest section of the Underground Railroad in Ohio. Returning to the days of his youth, he remembered the route as crossing the Ohio River near North Bend, then traveling upriver through the valley of the Great Miami River to the headwaters of the Auglaize River, through a Shawnee village now the city of Wapakoneta to Grand Rapids and ending by way of a route further north across Lake Erie to old Fort Malden, Canada. An overlay of this course on a present-day map of Ohio gives every indication this venerable artery traversed Shelby County.

North Bend, a small community located several miles downriver from Cincinnati, was a favored site of crossing because it contained more than a handful of safe-houses that functioned as overnight havens of rest, warmth and food. At least twenty runaway ports of entry existed along the full extent of the river forming the southern boundary of Ohio, but the extreme southwestern portion of the state early on took on the reputation as "the route to freedom." Crossings would commonly be made by means of skiff, canoe, raft or, on occasion an available log, and most often between the summer hours of sunset and sunrise. Passages were made, however, whenever opportunities were available. During the winter of 1856-1857 the UR experienced a thriving business due to the fact several hundred slaves were able to walk across the frozen Ohio at Cincinnati for a period of five full weeks.

Kentucky attempted in 1851 to close this portal-to-the-north by passing a law prohibiting the river passage of slaves by ferry operators, backed by a forfeiture of $200 plus an additional sum determined by the stated value of the slave. When a decision was made to build a bridge over the river at Cincinnati, the Bluegrass State, fearful the structure would present a golden opportunity for escape, rewrote the charter making the controlling board responsible for all slaves crossing without the permission of his or her owner. The Ohio legislature declined to offer its support.

Levi Coffin

Arriving on the north shore of the Ohio River, slaves were typically met by any one of an array of abolitionists ready and able to prepare them for their continued journey north. Some of the best known of this group were Josiah Hanson, the Reverend John Rankin, Harriet Beecher Stowe and, perhaps the most industrious of all, Levi Coffin, a Quaker by religion and businessman by trade who became known as "the president of the Underground Railroad" because of the thousands of slaves that passed through his care.

Coffin first sheltered fugitive slaves in his Fountain City, Indiana, home during the winter of 1826-1827. Twenty years later he moved his base of operations to Cincinnati and purchased a series of homes, settling finally on a large house on Wehrman Street where rooms were rented out to boarders. With guests moving in and out on a regular basis, the third floor was conveniently used as space where escaped slaves could be temporarily sheltered. Catherine Coffin periodically delivered food concealed in a large basket covered by a stack of freshly ironed linen.

One particular slave, Eliza Harris, had crossed the Ohio River when it was frozen over. When she arrived at the Coffin residence she was barefooted and nearly dead, but had strength enough left to tenderly grasp her baby in her arms. Provided with food, warm clothing and new shoes, she was able to continue her journey to freedom in Canada. Harriet Beecher Stowe was at the time living in the city and was acquainted with the Railroad activities of Levi and Catherine. Moved by this episode of rescue and escape to a new life, she retold it in her story of Uncle Tom's Cabin, an 1852 publication that eventually became the best-selling novel of the 19th century.

Levi Coffin died in 1877 at the age of 79. Historians estimate he aided more than 2,000 slaves in their flight to freedom. He placed the number closer to 3,000. When queried on why he was so involved in the abolitionist movement, he replied humbly that he believed it was always the proper thing to do.

By the 1840s several hundred slaves per year were successfully making their way north. Once in Ohio, however, they were not necessarily free. Although the state constitution forbade slavery, many citizens adhered to a pro-slavery sentiment. The Fugitive Slave Act of 1850 supported these attitudes by declaring that all runaways, upon capture, were to be returned to their southern owners. This aura of "free but not safe" was the reason the Underground Railroad continued to operate in a clandestine style and without any apparent degree of organization.

Many of the persons who guided the slaves from safe-house to safe-house along the many routes of the UR -- the so-called "conductors" -- became by necessity masters in the art of theatrical disguise. A wide array of clothes, accessories and makeup was commonly used to confuse the discerning eye of the "slave-catcher." A frequently used disguise was that of a Quaker woman, head tilted downward and outfitted with a high collar, long sleeves, gloves and a large sun-shielding hat. Males were dressed as females and females as men. In one celebrated case the runaway reached freedom costumed as a family nurse, complete with a rag-doll infant. In some communities the fugitives' worn and tattered clothing was repaired or even replaced by women organized into an UR-associated sewing circle.

If the contrivance of disguise was not practical then the art of concealment was employed. Escaping slaves were hidden in false bottoms of wagons and buried within loads of hay and even among lumpy sacks of potatoes. Transportation by covered wagon was a very common practice, especially when families were involved. One particular six-seated conveyance became widely known as "The Liberator" after it had reportedly transported fugitives hundreds and hundreds of miles throughout southwestern Ohio.

The Underground Railroad route north from Cincinnati was defined by a variety of passages, three of which involved Shelby County. The first followed the trace of the Miami and Erie Canal, the man-made water route that linked the Ohio River with Lake Erie, while the second was an overland course defined by the cities of Lebanon, Centerville, Dayton, Troy, Sidney, Wapakoneta, Ottawa, Grand Rapids and Toledo. The third, perhaps less used, route linked Sidney with Belle Center in Logan County and then ran to the northeast through Kenton, Tiffin and into the port city of Sandusky.  The canal route was a favorite of those individuals who could pay the cost of passage or who might earn passage by signing-on as a deckhand. For those fugitives strong of heart and muscle the cross-country route was chosen, but not advisedly as Dayton was suspected to be a hot-bed of pro-slavery sentiment and Railroad conductors avoided it whenever possible.

The records of the Ohio Historical Society in Columbus

contain information that give further description to Underground Railroad routes that approach and cross Shelby County. One account specifies the link that ran from Troy a distance of ten miles to Piqua where James Scudder helped the slaves onward to a site six miles northeast of Sidney where a station operated by James M. Roberts was located. Another account is an 1894 interview with Edward Walker, a former slave from Kentucky who was reported at the time to be one of the wealthiest residents of Windsor, Canada. After being temporarily caught in quicksand while crossing the Ohio River, Walker stayed in a safe-house in Cincinnati for a week and then left for Canada, along with his brother and his family, in a buggy driven by a white driver. Traveling at night up the valley of the Great Miami River they reached Bellefontaine and then rode the train to Sandusky where a ferryboat carried the group to Detroit.

The list of Shelby County abolitionists, while on the short side, is rather long if one considers the county population in 1840, the mid-point of the history of the UR, was only 12,153. In Sidney the roll call included David Edgar, John Wilson, Mrs. Eleanor Conklin, Mr. and Mrs. William McCullough, Judge A. J. Rebstock, Robert Given, Stephen Blanchard, Stephen Jefferson, James M. Roberts, John S. Bennett and, perhaps the most prominent of all, Pharoah A. Ogden, a licensed Wesleyan Methodist preacher as well as the editor of *The Sidney Journal* during the years of the Civil War. In the rural parts of the county the brothers

Thornton and Joseph Frye and John Odgen, brother of Pharoah, were active members of the Underground Railroad.

H. C. Roberts, the son of James M., recorded his family's early involvement in the Railroad in a 1895 interview. The younger Roberts' grandfather, William, left Virginia in 1814 with 21 of his 60 freed slaves for West Liberty, Ohio. Five years later, accompanied by four of his remaining slaves, William resettled in Port Jefferson following the outbreak of an epidemic of "trembles," an intestinal illness caused by drinking milk from cows who had fed on white snakeroot, a plant that contains the poison tremetol. H. C. recalled being wakened one winter night in 1850 by a knock on the door. He admitted four escapees, a woman and three men, who had secretly walked from Piqua in the company of two abolitionists. After being fed by his mother, whose name was Teresa, and her sister Mary Armstrong, they were directed along an old Indian trail to Lewistown, in Logan County, where James' brother Abel Roberts operated a safe house.

Whatever the particular route along the course of the Underground Railroad from the Ohio River to any of several Lake Erie ports, there was a network of safe-haven homes where runaway slaves were sure to find temporary shelter and help in getting to the next station. Once the fugitive traveler reached northern Ohio the end was in sight. Only one final barrier had to be taken to reach the "promised land" -- passage across Lake Erie.

Sandusky was a popular port of embarkation and home to a number of sympathetic boat captains. One individual by the name of Atwood offered free passage to many slaves on his steamboat "Arrow," and the skipper of the "Mayflower" carried so many escapee passengers on his laker it was eventually dubbed "The Abolition Boat."

Reports suggest few slaves ventured very far into the interior of Canada. Most of those who had successfully traveled the Railroad north from Cincinnati settled in the area of Ontario south of Windsor and west of Pelee Point. Amherstburg, the site of old Fort Malden, a British military station that dates to the earliest years of the 19th century, was the principal Lake Erie terminus of the UR in Canada. Here the former slave could establish residency on the "free soil" of Canada, as slavery had been declared unconstitutional there since 1803, the very same year Ohio was admitted into the Union.

Many, if not all, persons born in the environment of Southern slavery prior to the Civil War grew to maturity possessed by the concept of freedom. Some dreamed and some planned escape and thousands, driven by the hope of deliverance, actually succeeded in becoming "free men." The history of slavery in the United States is a sordid account of social servitude but, like any other episode of human bondage, it has its moments of enlightening courage and noble purpose. The story of the Underground Railroad and those many unsung heroes who maintained its operation is one such extended moment.

ONE MAN'S WAR

On the eve of the American Civil War, Ohio was in many aspects a divided state. Its burgeoning population included a number of powerful Republican politicians who believed in a strong central and undivided government that had to be preserved at any costs. On the other hand, many residents of counties forming the southern border of the Buckeye State opposed President Lincoln's policies by uniting under the label Peace Democrats, a faction hoping to indeed maintain a Union but without military intervention.

By and large, Ohio voters were solidly opposed to secession. Much of southern Ohio's economy, however, was dependent on open and transparent commerce with the slave states of Virginia and Kentucky. In addition, the position of the state between western agricultural interests and eastern manufacturing enterprises and its rank as the most wealthy state after Pennsylvania and New York were factors in establishing its degree of economic importance, while its recognized cultural diversity contributed to its political profile.

With the cannon shots in Fort Sumter, South Carolina, reverberating across the countryside, giving definition to the first day of war -- April 12, 1861 -- Ohio answered the call to duty and during the course of the next several years offered nearly 320,000 soldiers to the Union cause. The Buckeye State contributed the highest percentage of population of any northern state with 60 percent of all males between the ages of 18 and 45 wearing the blue uniform of the Grand Army of the Republic. Mostly volunteers, they were distributed among 230 regiments of infantry and cavalry, 25 light artillery batteries and nearly a dozen independent companies of sharpshooters.

Dozens of camps across the state trained and drilled the newly enlisted recruits, but the majority of the troops began their military experience at two posts; Camp Chase in Columbus and Camp Dennison near Cincinnati. Chase was established in May of 1861 as a training camp, a parole post and later as a prisoner-of-war camp. Then, rows of wooden huts lined up in military precision identified the location, but today it is marked by the graves of more than 2,000 Confederate soldiers at Camp Chase Cemetery in the Hilltop neighborhood of Columbus.

Dennison was a recruiting, training and medical post for the Union Army, constructed in April of 1861 not far from the juncture of the Little Miami River with the Ohio River on a site thought to be favored as an invasion route from the south. By summer, both camps were open for business and newspapers throughout Ohio were running advertisements stating recruiting offices were being opened in key communities. In Shelby County, *The Sidney Journal* advised its readers that the 20th Ohio Volunteer Infantry Regiment would be recruiting in Sidney.

Commonly listed as the 20th OVI, the 20th Ohio Volunteer Infantry was initially organized at Columbus in May of 1861, in response to President Lincoln's appeal for the enlistment of 75,000 volunteers interested in military service for a time period of three months. Ordered to western Virginia, the regiment saw action in minor engagements in June and July, before assuming sentry duty along the right-of-way of the Baltimore and Ohio Railroad. Its mandated duty time expired on August 23.

When the unit was reorganized in Columbus, the under-strength 20th traveled by rail to Camp Dennison on October 16 where it was assigned temporary quarters. Five days later, after being mustered into federal service for a period of three years, the recruits were marched to an auxiliary post, Camp King, where they began basic training. By mid-January 1862, the Regiment was bedded-down in winter quarters at Newport Barracks, Kentucky, where they spent their days guarding the Union batteries and earthworks around nearby Covington. On February 11, with the organizational roster attesting to full strength, the men boarded two steamboats and headed downriver for destinations unknown.

Over the next seven months the recruits of the 20th quickly became experienced soldiers. Their first baptism of fire occurred downstream to Dover, Tennessee, where the unconditional surrender of Fort Donelson gave the Union forces control of the Cumberland River. They acquired further laurels as part of the Army of the Tennessee under Major General Ulysses S. Grant, which engaged the Confederate forces in June at the Battle of Shiloh for strategic control of the headwaters of the Tennessee River. The summer of 1862 found the men mostly on guard duty in and around Bolivar, Tennessee, and then they traveled by rail to Corinth, Mississippi, to rejoin the rest of Grant's army. By the first week in October, the 20th was in need of rest, having chased the Rebel forces back and forth across the Tennessee-Mississippi state line with minimal success. Reduced in strength by death, battlefield confusion and a growing list of men wounded in action, the 20th sought new recruits.

On October 1, 1862, a 38-year-old, blue-eyed, dark-skinned, six-foot-tall Shelby County farmer answered the call to duty by swearing allegiance to the United States and signing his X at the recruiting office in Sidney. Designated with the rank of "Recruit," George Deal was assigned to Company K of the 20th OVI and sent to Camp Dennison. Three weeks later, he mailed the first of many letters -- written for him by a fellow soldier, since George could neither read nor write -- to the rural home of his wife and three children in Montra, the crossroads village located north of Port Jefferson;

> Camp Dennison. October 23. Dear Wife. With pleasure, I set myself to write you a few lines to let you know I am well and enjoying good health. Capt. Updegraff wrote a letter to Mr. Thomas Robardson to let you have anything you wanted out of his (grocery) store. We have drew our uniforms and have no money and we don't know when we will get it and we don't know when we will leave here but not until we get our bounty money.

For the next ten weeks George was in continual doubt as to his role in the developing events of the Civil War. He had become a soldier and like soldiers of all wars he was living on hope, rumor and expectation -- and more rumor;

> Camp Dennison. November 9. Dear Wife. We expect to be paid next Thursday and if that is the case I want you to call at the Express office on next Saturday. I shall endever to send (money) there and you can call and get it next Saturday. We intend to leave for Tennessee as soon as we get our money. We have been having some good times here it is nice soldiering here for my party. My feet is well. I can stand marching with the best of them.

§ § § §

> Camp Dennison. December 5. Dear Wife. We received our $13 this morning and ten of which I paid to the Captain. The remaining three I will keep for my own use. We will leave tomorrow evening or on Monday next for the regiment without fail. We go by the boat from Cincinnati to Columbus, Ky and no doubt the trip will be interesting one and full of novelty to me at least as I have never been on the river.

§ § § §

> South of Cincinnati. December 14. Dear Wife. I left camp on last Monday and took the cars for Cincinnati and there we took the steamboat for Memphis, Tennessee. I am in good heart. I think it won't be long till I will come home for sure is a great talk of peace. I would like writing to you but I can't write and therefore I must get some one to write for me.

§ § § §

> Columbus, KY. January 2, 1863. Dear Wife. We have been at this place two weeks and no telling when we will get away. We was called out in line of battle on the 24 last month. We remained in line two days and nights but no enemy came. . .you see we spent Christmas in the line of battle. I like soldiering very well. The

captain says we will be paid next week if we are paid off you may expect some money soon.

§ § § §

Lafayette, TN. January 14. Dear Wife. We expect to leave here soon for Memphis. We got to the regiment the 10th of this month. We have been taking the round but have not got in any fight yet and we may not. When we want meat we go out and press in a hog or a beef and never ask the price of it. I have done some little marching and find I will have to throw away part of my load it more than I can carry.

Finally, now promoted to the rank of private, George Deal was able to join up with the main body of the 20th OVI. His first real encounter with war occurred in the Battle of Raymond, followed by the Battle of Champion Hill, both preliminary engagements that took place before the siege of the city of Vicksburg, Mississippi, in the summer of 1863;

Camp Vicksburg. July 6, 1863. We have gained the great victory at last. Vicksburg was surrendered up on the fourth of July . . . with 35,400 prisoners besides what was killed and wounded. For further particulars I can't write.

Bloodied, battered and now much the wiser about the realities of mortal conflict, the men of the 20th assumed reserve status until the spring of the following year, when they received the very best of news -- the regiment was going home for a one-month furlough. *The Sidney Journal* recorded the details on April 1, 1864:

These war torn soldiers marched into town, and around the Public Square, preceded by their splendid brass band, with their tattered flags flying . . . they halted in front of Carey's Hall . . . and were briefly addressed in words of appropriate commendation and welcome.

On the 9th of May, his visit home completed, George Deal resumed his campaign of communication:

Dear Companion Sarah Deal. I stayed the night I left at Thorns tavern in Sidney and got about the cars the next morning and arrived at Cincinnati . . . at which place I (have) overtaken the regiment. Arrived at Cairo yesterday morning . . . but it is a probability that we will not stay here very long till we leave for Huntsville.

Two weeks later, George wrote Sarah in words that spoke of uncertainty:

We left Cairo . . . came by way of Clifton, Tennessee . . . to Molesburg . . . from there to Pulaski . . . and then started for Huntsville. So we will stay here 2 days and then go to Dolton, Georgia . . . in order to join General Sherman. You need not look for any more letters for some time as we are on a march and will be for some two or three months yet and so I have no chance to write.

On the 21st of July, the boys of Shelby County, along with other elements of the Army of the Tennessee, routed a Confederate division and occupied the slopes of Leggitt's Hill, a strategic location from which Union artillery could easily shell the city of Atlanta. Retiring for the night in reinforced fortifications, the victors expected a period of rest and relaxation.

Shelby County reenactors of the 94th OVI. *Photo compliments of Shelby County Historical Society.*

The next day, however, an atmosphere of haze and heat enveloped the countryside laden with expectations of trouble. Then, just after the noon hour, the first shell fell and the Battle of Atlanta was under way. Eleven hours later the field of battle before the 20th OVI was littered with the bodies of 600 enemy fighters. The casualties of the 20th were listed as 33 dead, 47 wounded and 56 missing in action. Private George Deal was initially listed as "missing in action," but a later investigation confirmed his death "while in the line of his duty."

As was the custom with the armies of both the North and the South, the dead were quickly buried in graves dug at the exact location in which the bodies were found. Inscribed markers, generally made of a scrap of wood, listed pertinent information and identified the gravesite. The body of Private Deal was found lying between the remains of Private Felix W. Baird, Company B, 78th OVI and those of Private William N. Smith, Company D, 20th OVI.

Several years later, the dead of the Battle of Atlanta were removed to permanent graves within the grounds of the newly dedicated Marietta National Cemetery. An upright stone of Vermont marble marked the graves of Privates Baird and Smith, but the wooden marker for the body that had lain between them on the field of battle was missing, the possible victim of decay or theft. Those remains were thus buried and marked with a marble stone that bore the simple words UNKNOWN U. S. SOLDIER, one of 3,048 Union "unknowns" buried on a hilltop off the corner of Cole Street and Washington Avenue in downtown Marietta, Georgia.

For the better part of a century and a-half, the three remains lay side by side in Section E: site 5815, Felix W. Baird; site 5816, UNKNOWN; site 5817, William N. Smith. Then, through the labors and interests of Brad Quinlin, a Marietta-based Civil War historian and researcher, the identity of the remains of George Deal was finally determined and verified. After thoroughly reviewing, checking and cross-checking the records of original burial, the locations of military units during the Battle of Atlanta and rosters of the dead from each regiment, Quinlin presented definitive proof George Deal was the sole 20th OVI soldier who fought in the Battle of Atlanta whose grave could not be found in the Marietta cemetery. The UNKNOWN of site 5816 was indeed that of Private George Deal of Shelby County.

In 1878, three years after the completion of the Monumental Building in Sidney, Ohio, a polished marble "Heroes Tablet" was dedicated and placed on permanent display on the second floor. Among the 309 names of the fallen, each inscribed in gold lettering, is that of George Deal. From a series of letters written for him to his wife and children back home in Montra, the facts of his involvement in the Civil War are well known. Now the details regarding exactly where this one man's war ended and who his comrades were during his very last moment of life are also known. George Deal can finally Rest in Peace.

THE BOYS OF '98

It took place almost twelve decades ago, lasted for 109 days and involved 109 officers and enlisted men from Shelby County, tested America's concept of manifest destiny, helped a cowboy from the Dakota Badlands gain access to the White House and was labeled a "splendid little war" by a one-time Secretary of State. Although largely forgotten today, the Spanish-American War marked the emergence of the United States as a world power and triggered a national debate over the cost and value of expansionism.

The Spanish-American War of 1898 was the result of American intervention in the Cuban War of Independence. War clouds had gathered before, in 1873 over the Virginius Affair, a diplomatic squabble with Great Britain and Spain involving a rag-tag group of Cuban insurrectionists, and then more recently when American yellow journalism was directed toward the perceived inadequacy of the Spanish administration of Cuba. The main issue, of course, was Cuban independence, but a secondary concern lay in the fact that positioned but 90 miles off the Florida coast Cuba was too close to the eastern border of America for advocates of the Monroe Doctrine. The war was fought in two theatres; the southwest Pacific and the Caribbean.

The trouble began at precisely 9:40 PM Tuesday, February 15, 1898, when the 324-foot long, 6,682-ton battleship USS Maine blew up and sank into the mud of Havana harbor, leaving her main deck armament of four 10-inch guns, capable of firing 520-pound shells a distance of 20,000 yards, fully submerged and forever silenced. Exactly two months later the U. S. Congress declared war against Spain, giving purposeful intent to the much-ballyhooed rallying call "Remember the Maine and To Hell With Spain."

In Shelby County, the men of Company L, Third Infantry Regiment, Ohio National Guard responded to the call for action. Organized in 1881 as Company D, the unit had over the years been twice called to duty in Cincinnati "to assist in suppressing riot and incendiarism." Now, under the command of Captain William T. Amos and reorganized as Company L, a full cadre of 75 men, clothed in outdated uniforms and armed with modern Springfield rifles, left Sidney by train on April 26, 1898, bound for Camp Bushnell, Columbus, where two weeks later they were mustered into federal service. Left behind at the depot were 5,000 "fathers, mothers, sisters, wives and sweethearts" who, the *Sidney Daily News* reported, had bid them "God speed and a safe return in the most patriotic demonstration ever witnessed in our city and never excelled anywhere."

In Columbus, physical exams were under way with mixed and bothersome results. According to a report sent to the local press "each Company contained a number of weak-kneed men, from six up to twenty or more (who) in many instances . . . were hooted and drummed out of camp . . . but when the time came . . . not for a moment did a single man (of Company L) waver." These acts of overt derision were quickly followed by a subtle form of discrimination that became evident when a new order stipulated 72 men, rather than 75, now constituted a full company. Included in the roster of three to be returned to Shelby County was the entire compliment of Company L "colored cooks who (had) so efficiently served the Company for the past three years . . . and were the sickest men in camp when they learned they would not be permitted to enlist in the U. S. service."

Military camp experience, regardless of the branch of service, is typically a matter of "hurry up and wait," and so it was at Camp Bushnell as organization slowly became the order of the day. The men received new uniforms, complete with an iconic colored slouch hat and a pay rate of $2 per day. In due time all the revolvers that were the individual property of the enlisted men were collected and sent home to the owners' households. When the troops were not on guard duty or not cleaning their rifles their days were spent in perfecting the art of coordinated drill, washing clothes, snacking on the contents of food baskets received from home and catching up on "the latest war news" in newspapers brought to camp by visitors.

On May 1, Commodore George Dewey, commander-in-chief of the U. S. Navy's Asiatic Squadron, handily defeated an entire Spanish squadron in Manila Bay at the cost of a mere nine wounded sailors. With this victory, America began to build a two-ocean naval force and with minimal fanfare sought increasing responsibility for the maintenance of peace on an international basis. Closer to home, Assistant Secretary of the Navy Theodore Roosevelt argued for land intervention in Cuba and convinced the U. S. Army to raise an all-volunteer force -- the 1st Volunteer Cavalry. Roosevelt resigned his position and enlisted in this 1,060-man group of college athletes, cowboys and ranchers, soon known far and wide as the "Rough Riders."

In mid-May, a contingent of visitors to Camp Bushnell included Drs. H.E. Beebe and A. W. Reddish, no doubt inspecting cleanliness and health conditions; Miss Margaret Lanpher, intent unstated; and, his notebook and pencil in hand, William Binkley, editor of *The Sidney Journal*, in search of a lead story for the next Friday's edition.

Weeks of orientation and training in Columbus came to an end with the announcement that an advance force of several hundred men versed in Spanish and acquainted with the island topography were en route to Cuba. With this move underway, the entire mass of American volunteers began to move south into assembly bases in southern Florida.

Assigned to Camp De Sota, nearby Tampa on the site where the famous explorer made a landing on his tour of discovery in the 16th century, men of the Shelby County contingent were initially enthralled by their assigned beach location but soon were grousing the "air is filled with white sand . . . and coming in contact with a person who is perspiring this fine sand and dirt sticks like glue." Like soldiers everywhere, they also were complaining they "know little of what is going on in the outside world." Bored with a routine of drill and camp cleanup

Colonel Theodore Roosevelt, commander of the Rough Riders.

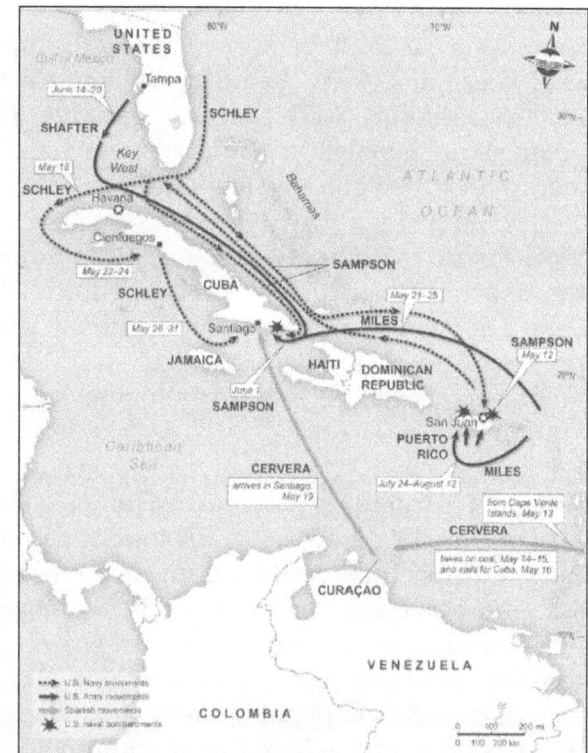

Caribbean Theater, Spanish American War May to August 1898

exercises, they spent off-duty hours bathing in the ocean and hunting for alligators in the surrounding swamps.

Soon, however, activities at the Company L camp were in full swing. Horses were loaded onto the transport "Florida," all the officers had purchased Colt revolvers at a cost of $15 each and rumors kept the enlisted men in a high state of alert and anxiety. Then came the orders and disappointment -- there will be a delay awaiting further developments.

Meanwhile, back in Sidney, efforts were under way to recruit an additional 37 men, enough to bring the roster of Company L up to the newly approved level of 109 personnel. Following assembly at the Grand Army of the Republic Hall, the recruits were marched to the armory for physical examinations and basic drill exercises. Within a matter of days, the new complement was at full roster, composed of young men from throughout the county; Jackson Center, Anna, Ballou, Port Jefferson, Oran and Hardin. With the city in "holiday attire . . . and flags and bunting on display from almost every business house and residence," a send-off dance held in the armory on the evening of Tuesday the 21st of June featured music furnished by the Regal Mandolin Club.

The next afternoon, following a swearing in ceremony, the boys boarded a special Cincinnati, Hamilton and Dayton rail car for a "run straight through to Tampa." In addition to personal items, a great load of provisions and articles most needed in camp, donated by citizens and a who's who list of local merchants, was added to the fully-loaded rail car. Included in the bonanza of goodies was a case of cove oysters from the Robinson Grocery Company, a box of pickled fish from Henry Albers, a case of canned peaches from Piper Brothers, ten pounds of mettwurst from John Steinle, a bundle of towels from I. H. Thedieck, one box of lead pencils from C. J. Briggs, a large box of soap from Robert Enders and six dozen handkerchiefs from N. C. DeWeese and Sons, in addition to numerous contributions of cigars, stogies and various quantities of chewing and smoking tobacco.

At full strength, Company L longed for orders giving them opportunity for action against the Spanish enemy. Instead, the days now became a routine of boredom and contrived activities: collecting sea shells along the beach: chartering a sail boat: gathering and cracking hickory nuts: writing letters home: and in the case of Freeman Wright, falling asleep in the woods and missing the 9:00 o'clock roll call. Three times they had been under orders to "move out" -- to Santiago, then to Jacksonville and then again to Santiago -- and just as many times the orders were countermanded.

Every now and then, mock battles were arranged, and the troops, firing blank cartridges, fought their way "up to the supposed enemy over palmetto roots, through barbed wire fences and undergrowth in some places five feet high but all the boys enjoyed it."

In late June, units of the American Army began to probe the enemy strength in Cuba in a series of skirmishes during which the tide of battle gradually shifted from inexperience to Yankee success. On July 1, a combined force of infantry and cavalry regiments, along with the Rough Riders under the command of Colonel Roosevelt, stormed the north-south oriented San Juan Hill, two miles outside of Santiago. Over 200 Americans died in this, the bloodiest and most famous battle of the war, compared to less than 60 on the Spanish side, but the view from the crest of the hill gave great advantage to the U. S. forces when they began the siege of Santiago.

Still the lads from Shelby County were being held in mainland reserve. On an almost daily basis hospital ships arrived at Port Tampa loaded with the wounded, the most serious of whom were moved immediately to facilities at Atlanta. Stories of bravery abounded. One man had been shot five times but "was as lively and jovial as ever . . . others in the arms, breast, and in fact in every part of the body."

Many troops reported the Springfield rifle to be a flawed weapon, because the smoke produced by its firing gave the enemy a perfect target. Among the reported list of deaths was one Joseph French of Sidney, a member of the Sixth Cavalry, but further inquiry proved the report to be false, a mix-up with another soldier of the same name.

The *Sidney Daily News* headline of July 14 said it all -- "SANTIAGO IS OURS. The City Surrendered To-Day After All Hope Had Been

Given Up By the Spaniards." An announcement from the White House indicated General Yose Toral had accepted the demand of an unconditional surrender following a ten-day siege of the city. For all intents and purposes, the war over, but still the troopers of Company L lounged outside Tampa. Not for long.

On August 1, the tents were folded and packed and the entire troop made preparation to move to Fernandina, a community of 4,000 located on an island on the Atlantic side of Florida, a mere three miles south of the Georgia state line. At first reported as a healthier place than Tampa, the grounds assigned to Company L were soon recognized as an overgrown field inundated with lizards, thousand-leg spiders, ants, bugs, beetles of every description, hundreds of snakes and "mosquitoes by the millions."

With little to do but stay out of trouble, life at Fernandina took on a routine similar to that of all armies following the end of battle, and rumor ran rampant. Some swore the next order would take them to Puerto Rico, others believed they would be assigned occupation duty in Cuba, a few feared they could be sent to garrison duty at Manila, but the majority were thinking they would soon be heading for home. The majority were correct. On September 2, the War Department ordered the Third Ohio Volunteer Infantry Regiment to proceed home as soon as possible, via Camp Wheeler at Huntsville, Alabama. Apparently these orders had been anticipated, since the *Sidney Daily News* reported Company L "left Fernandina at 3 o'clock Monday afternoon (August 29) and got into Huntsville this morning (August 31) at 2 o'clock." After a stay of a little over two weeks in Alabama, they began the final segment of the long trip home. On Saturday, September 17, "the members of Company L, Third Ohio Infantry, arrived home from the war this morning at 10:45 o'clock." It had been 144 days since they had left Sidney bound for Camp Bushnell.

In the aftermath of celebration, there was much speculation as to why Company L was never ordered into battle. As the press reported, "the boys came out to fight . . . and at Tampa their expectations were worked up to fever heat." After an investigation, it was found the lack of transportation was the cause. It seems the Third Regiment had been scheduled for action and its horses already loaded, but the ramming of one transport by another involved the very ship assigned to the members of Company L.

On Thursday, August 5, 1905, the first reunion of the "Boys of '98" brought 40 of the original 109 members to the Tawawa Lake Boathouse, in the eastern section of Sidney. The "army-style" dinner consisted of roast beef, beans with boiled bacon, Irish potatoes, brown gravy and "a few plates of hard tack to serve as a relish." W.T. Amos, the commanding officer of Company L, gave a short history of the hometown unit and announced that since "muster out . . . three times only has death broken the ranks of the company." Plans were announced concerning the formation of a branch of Spanish American War Veterans, and soon thereafter the men bid their fairwells and then gradually faded away into the pages of history.

The Spanish American War has also faded away into the annals of history, but its conclusion brought change to the world. The 1898 Treaty of Paris gave America temporary control of Cuba, and indefinite authority over the island nation of Puerto Rico, the Pacific island of Guam, and the entirety of the Philippine Islands.

RETURN OF THE DOUGHBOYS

Not long after the War Department had released the statement, its' wording had been set in bold print on the inside page of the January 15, 1919, issue of the *Sidney Daily News*: NEAR HALF OF 37TH WAS LOST IN BATTLES. The reference was, of course, to the 37th Infantry Division, the National Guard unit that called Ohio home, thus its nickname the "Buckeye Division."

Six months earlier advance units, composed mainly of headquarters personnel, had arrived at Brest, France, to set the stage for the division's entry into World War I. Now the troops -- or "doughboys" as they preferred to be called -- were returning to America, scarred by the elements of war. According to Colonel Robert L Hubler, of the 27,000 men of the 37th who saw action, only 15,000 remained when Germany signed the armistice, effective on the 11th hour of the 11th day of the 11th month of 1918. Almost all of the division's equipment had been lost and only 40 trucks of the 361 originally issued were still operational. In addition, of the 4,000 horses with which the division had been equipped, less than 1,500 were still alive.

During the 77 days spent at the front line, the men of Ohio had advanced 19 miles and captured nearly 1,500 German soldiers. These successes were, however, marked by a casualty report that read of pain, death and confusion. The loss of life totaled 1,066, while those wounded in battle tallied up to 4,321. Finally, during its time in France the 37th

had received nearly 7,000 replacements, the result of illnesses and the continuing need to transfer troops to other American units as the battlefront meandered back and forth across the landscape of western Europe.

Of the four regiments that constituted the total roll call of the 37th Division, the 148th contained the majority of those Shelby County boys who had answered the call to duty. Following a designated period of basic training at Camp Sheridan, Alabama, and its transport to Europe, the division distinguished itself through five distinct infantry and tank-driven drives, three taking place in France and two in Belgium. Now it was packing its equipment for its return to civilian life on home soil.

Such preparations couldn't begin soon enough for the folks in Shelby County. When the first news arrived on Thursday, January 16, 1919, Corporal William (Happy) Fair sent a telegram to his mother in Sidney that he would be home "in a day or two." Delayed by the necessity of red tape, he finally made it on the 27th and soon was sharing his wartime experiences. One particular engagement he had been involved in was the stuff of genuine warfare.

As he related it, all was in readiness when the second hand identified the appointed moment and the regiment leapt out of the trenches and went "over the top" in a sustained drive against the German forces

encamped in the dense foliage of the Argonne Forest. Full of vim and vigor, they advanced until an enveloping cloud of mustard gas put some of the men out of the fighting. Happy being one of them and recovering, he continued to lead his men until stopped by a bullet in his right arm and another in the right hip. He was discharged with a 20 percent disability.

For others, the ending was not so hopeful. The high school auditorium was filled to overflowing for the Sunday afternoon commemoration services for three local boys who would not be coming home. The silence was overwhelming each time a fallen soldier was eulogized: Lieutenant Frederick N. Annandale of Sidney: Corporal Raymond G. Nettleship of Port Jefferson and Corporal Emerson Heineman, born in Auglaize County but inducted into service in Sidney. Judge Charles M. Wyman spoke for all when he intoned: "The war of liberation, my friends, being o'er, we now count the cost."

The holiday season came and went and still there was no word from the War Department when the main body of the 37th would be arriving home. The soldiers had been assured, however, that their division would be kept intact "in order that it might parade in one or more of the larger cities of the Buckeye State to show the 'home folks' what the fighting boys look like when they are in trim to scrap with the unspeakable Hun."

During the last week of January 1919, Pat Malone came home and gave every indication he was ready and eager to tell "the story of his life in the army with much enthusiasm." His service dated back to 1916 when his regiment was ordered to Texas to protect its citizens against the border raids of the notorious bandit Doroteo Arango, alias Francisco "Pancho" Villa. When Pat returned to Camp Perry, Ohio, he was reassigned to duty with the American Expeditionary Force and transport to France.

By the summer of 1918 Malone was engaged in battle in the Chateau Thierry sector of France where, in their first real battle of World War I, the U. S. forces subdued a major German offensive aimed toward the capture of Paris. When the smoke and noise had dissipated, the American Army tallied 67,000 casualties, one of which was trooper

Malone. Wounded in the shoulder and nose by a bursting shell, he spent weeks in a base hospital before being discharged.

Arriving home at about the same time as Pat Malone, Charles W. Tucker of Jackson Center had a different tale to tell. After basic training he was assigned as a crewmember of a mammoth Railway Battery gun, one of the largest in the world with a 65-foot-long barrel and a weight of 98 tons. Tilted at an angle of 45 degrees, it could fire a 14-inch shell weighing 1,450 pounds a distance of 50 miles. In talks with the local press, he modestly acknowledged he was "gassed while over there" and that at one time he was on constant duty for 100 hours and unable to change his clothes for a period of three weeks.

By the time Sergeant Elmer Weipert spoke to the reporters, the residents of Sidney and Shelby County could begin to sense some similarity -- a record of hard and continued fighting on the battlefronts of western Europe. He related the terror of going "over the top three times in three days" in late September of 1918. It was on the morning of the 29th that he received his wound, in the knee when a high explosive "minnewarfer" detonated near him. Taken first to a field aid station and then to a hospital at Vichy, France, he landed at Hoboken, New Jersey, was discharged at Camp Sherman, Chillicothe, and sent home to Sidney, his war service completed.

The reports of Sidney and Shelby County servicemen, combined with evidences of their unusual bravery in battle, explain why the 37th was one of only two American divisions chosen to parade in Brussels after the Germans had evacuated the city. The Buckeye Division was becoming famous.

The first contingent of men, some 13,000 strong, sailed from Hoboken on June 16, 1918, on the confiscated German liner "Leviathan." After initial assembly in the trenches at Bourmont, a mountain hamlet made famous by Joan of Arc, they underwent their baptism of fire during an air raid at Baccarat, a commune in northeastern France where, for more than 200 years, the worlds' finest luxury crystal ware had been manufactured. By mid-September the unit had occupied the fields of Verdun, sustained a drive that gave them their first taste of fame and captured a strongly fortified sector of the front defined by the villages of Ivory, Cierges and Mount Faucon.

Transferred to Belgium the 37th fought at Denterghen, forded the Lys River and advanced beyond the shores of the Scheldt River, liberating more than 20 towns along the way. Preparing for yet another attack, they received orders to cease hostilities effective the late morning of November 11. The war was over and the troops began preparations for their long voyage home to Ohio.

On time, at 9:10 PM the Western Ohio rolled to a stop opposite the fire hall in the Monument Building and 13, crisply uniformed soldiers exited, the first announced group of local men to arrive home from war. They had already been mustered out of service at Camp Sherman, and were now officially civilians again. Members of Company H, 329th Regiment of the 83rd Infantry Division -- the Ohio Division -- the other military unit historically linked to the Buckeye State, they were quickly enveloped by the assembled crowd. It was Saturday, February 15, 1919, and Sergeants Dean, Pruden, Offenbacker, Gerstner, Wiant and Shepherd; Corporals Shatto, Lorton, Brown, Wagner, Costollo; Cook Kysenceder and Bugler Bolheimer were home. With the fire bell ringing in the background, an impromptu parade of cheering persons began to march around the square, coming to an end at the Wagner House corner.

Two and one-half weeks later, ladies of more than a handful of churches sponsored a community dinner, for almost 200 attendees, honoring the returned soldiers in the dining hall of the Methodist Church. While the evening was declared a success, it became apparent that festivities of a more formal and official nature had to be organized. Community leaders decided the upcoming Fourth of July celebration was the time for the city and county to pay tribute to a growing list of fallen and returning heroes.

As winter slowly phased into spring, memorials and tributes were organized on a continuing basis, both near and afar. The *Sidney Daily News* reported the crowds that packed every square yard of the Hoboken pier on Friday, March 28, contained "residents of every section of central and western Ohio. . .almost every town had someone present." This arrival had special significance, for the big liner "St. Louis" contained the principal elements of the 148th, the regiment full of those who commonly called the upper Great Miami River valley home. Unfortunately, their demobilization process via Camp Mills, New York and Camp Sherman kept them from attending Arbor Day services during which Sidney High School students planted six elm trees along the north side of the schoolyard "in memory of the pupils who have died in service."

With victory against the dreaded Hun firmly embedded in the history books, America now turned to the task of expected post-war activities, those events that would spell fini to the horror and tragedy of human conflict. With realization the war had to be paid for, a statewide Victory Loan operation was organized and Shelby County learned its quota had been set at an even $448,000. This "debt" was distributed among 14 townships and the City of Sidney, with publicity handled by Mrs. Ralph Kah and Mrs. H. A. Amos.

Sunday, May 4, was designated Victory Loan Sunday, with churches throughout the state making a special appeal for the contribution of "loan" monies, some of which would be used to help feed a war-torn Europe. For those who did not make church a part of their weekly ritual, much ado was made of the planned arrival of a 'Whippet' tank, which would locally "be put though the paces. . .to boost the Victory Loan." If this were not enough encouragement toward support of the

Loan, arrival of a "trophy train" was scheduled to arrive at the Big Four depot on Thursday, April 24, for a five-hour period during which "many of the trophies captured by the American soldiers in France and Belgium" would be on display.

The Mark A Whippet tank proved to be a great success. The six-ton, tracked, British-designed vehicle, armed with four Hotchkiss MK-1 machine guns rolled into town, noisily cranked its way around the square and then maneuvered along East Court Street to Gramercy Park where an "exhibition was given and feats performed that were seemingly incredible." After all the dust and noise had subsided, one member of the immense crowd was quoted as saying the Whippet could "climb a pole if necessary."

Two weeks after the Whippet left town, headed for Bellefontaine and yet another gee-whiz demonstration, townspeople learned that "Shelby County has 'gone over the top' in the Victory Loan drive." The expected quota had been exceeded by $12,200.

Finally, the day arrived for the big Welcome Home and Fourth of July parade. The program committee had been meeting regularly for weeks, and the city was gaily decorated with flags and red-white-and-blue bunting. Streets within a block of the public square were roped off, and the parade participants began to assemble on West Poplar Street. The parade was not up to planned expectation, but the crowds were nevertheless noisy and the weather was cooperative. Three bands, from Sidney, Degraff and Wapakoneta, were interspersed with marchers who represented the Tawawa Tribe of Red Men, the Junior United American Mechanics and the Wagner Manufacturing Company. Various businesses sponsored floats: Sidney Home Telephone Company, Peerless Bread Machine Company, Mull Woodwork Company, Sidney Rug Works, Steinle's Stove and Tin Store and the Cherry Cheer soda fountain syrup company.

Downtown activities started with the opening salute at 6 AM and concluded with late-night dancing "on the pavilion on the northeast corner of the square." Festivities continued throughout the day; acrobatics, balloon ascensions, band concerts, buffalo dances and ball games, interspersed with "curious Japanese daylight fireworks showing birds, flowers, animals and fish floating in the air." Unfortunately, the Kentucky barbecue concession was not well patronized, supposedly due to its location on north Miami Avenue away from the crowds. Shortly after sunset a bomb was detonated to alert the public the nighttime fireworks would soon begin --"for two solid hours the heavens will be illuminated with prismatic torrents of brilliant fire."

For Sidney and Shelby County the "War to End All Wars" was over. Armed with abilities hopefully up to par with their ambitions the residents of the Great Miami River watershed looked forward to their future. Ahead lay the Roaring Twenties, the Great Depression and World War II. But then, that is another story.

CITY & COUNTY INNOVATIONS

Long before that frontier moment when the first stake was pounded into the ground, Sidney was gifted with an outstanding geographic bloodline. Its latitude identified a location mid-way between tropical heat and Arctic ice, and its longitude gave it association with a virgin forest firmly anchored in mineral-rich, glacial soil. Game, fish and fowl abounded, and the seasons came and went on an equal basis. Perhaps the best attribute of all was the presence of a river, called the Msimiyamithipi by the Shawnee and Riviere à la Roche by the French. Early settlers chose the name Great Miami after the Algonquian-speaking people who had inhabited the region for centuries.

Throughout the Miami River valley Native Americans traded wares and fought wars. Later, the valley became the focus of the Miami-Erie Canal, then in succession a rail and traction line, the Dixie Highway and finally Interstate 75. Early on, flatboat transport delivering agricultural commodities to New Orleans even brought Shelby County river commerce.

Livestock grazed on the courthouse pasture, landscaping was scarce, gravel walkways sufficed, and piles of manure spoiled the roads, until eventually Sidney became environmentally aware. When hard times arrived, a federal conservation program brought the improvement of farmland drainage that added to the welfare of many rural families and also helped numerous unemployed and out-of-hope young men. Months later, when federal financing brought electricity, a glow of optimism seemed to settle across the countryside.

Through it all, the people remained resilient and welcomed every new concept, be it the onset of trans-continental airmail or the arrival of a hometown derby. To this day, innovation continues, ever challenging, yet ever hopeful.

ANTEBELLUM RIVER COMMERCE

The history of the mode, means and courses of surface-based travel across the length and breadth of the North American continent is a subject that would, in print form alone, require a space capable of containing thousands of references. From that distant day when the first settler stepped ashore along the eastern seaboard through yesterday, travelers and planners have sought ever newer routes that would allow safe, convenient and economic passage from point A to point B. Native Americans found the very first courses by following ancient paths worn by immeasurable generations of wildlife migrating between feeding and breeding grounds. Wagon travel required the expansion of paths into dirt roads, improved here and there by corduroy reinforcement, which eventually evolved into two-lane and then interstate all weather highways. Wherever moving water was encountered, multiple means of transport became available, progressing from canoe, pirogue, flatboat, keelboat and steamboat, to modern-day barge and towboat movement. Not to be forgotten is the era of canal construction, beginning around 1810 and ending some three decades later when railroads extended into literally every nook and cranny of the country.

The prosperity of Shelby County is closely tied to this history of transportation in America. A major Shawnee and Miami tribal trade and migration route linking the valleys of the Alleghany Mountains to the Great Lakes followed the course of the Great Miami River and Loramie Creek. This same course was employed by horse-drawn stagecoaches, and later by donkey- horse- and oxen-drawn boats along the 300-mile-long Miami and Erie Canal that conveniently connected the river city of Cincinnati to the booming lake port of Toledo. During the 1850s, steel rails and steam locomotives traveling both north-to-south and east-to-west connected farm and community to coastal industrial cities as distant as New Orleans and New York City. Today, the once famous Dixie Highway is relegated to the status of a county byway, while the four- to six- lane-wide, 1,786 mile long Interstate 75 links Sault Ste. Marie, Michigan with Hialeah, Florida, via Shelby County.

Once the crests of the Pennsylvania mountains had been conquered by waves of migrants -- farmers, adventurers, miners, cattlemen and trappers -- seeking fortune and a new life, the preferred way of travel changed from horse and wagon to the waters of the western flowing Ohio River and its tributaries. As early as the mid-1760s a boat construction industry plied its trade at the confluence of the Monongahela and Alleghany Rivers, today the site of the city of Pittsburgh. Crafts of every dimension and description were readily available for the right price. Paddle- propelled canoes and pirogues were the easiest and the cheapest to build but their capacity for cargo and passengers was limited.

A more efficient means of transportation was inaugurated in 1811, when the 148-foot long, 370 ton steamboat New Orleans -- the first such craft built for Ohio River travel -- carried 60 passengers downstream to its namesake city in a voyage that took 82 days. Several other steamboats arrived over the next several years, but the average life of these early crafts was but three years, the result of sinking by river snags, explosions and technologies that were yet to be perfected. Until these problems could be overcome, the preferred choice of large volume transportation down the Ohio River and many of its major tributaries was a class of boat that filled the gap between the one- or two- man propelled canoe and the pilot-controlled steamboat. This category of river craft included both the flatboat and the keelboat.

As their name implies, keelboats were constructed around a stability-providing keel, the backbone of a craft that extends from bow to stern and around which frames are attached. These boats were generally narrow, cigar-shaped and ranged in length from 50 to 80 feet with a width that approximated one-third their length. They drew 2-3 feet of water when fully loaded, and thus could be maneuvered in smaller rivers, tributaries and shallow lakes. Employed primarily to transport cargo, they were designed to move both downstream and upstream, although moving a keelboat against the current was extremely difficult.

Either oars or poles were usually used to travel upstream. To pole a keelboat, crew members, up to 24 men on the larger boats, walked along a runway from bow to stern pushing against a pole pressed against the river bottom. In faster current, towlines were manhandled from the shore. Keelboats may have had a sail or a cabin located mid-ship, but they were also built with an open deck. In their time they were the regular packet boats of the larger rivers, and they were making their way on smaller tributaries as late as 1855. Because coordinated efforts were required to move upstream, keelboat crews were more professional and worked together longer than those on other river craft. Residents of the riverbank communities they visited, however, considered them boisterous in every conceivable manner. Both ashore and onboard, the men were equally ready to fight an opponent or dance a tune to the music of a fiddle. Historians believe the first keelboat was built on the Ohio River, at Fort Pitt, in 1768.

Meriwether Lewis had a keelboat built to his own design in Elizabeth, Pennsylvania, the center of the early boat industry on the Monongahela River, for his famous 1803-1806 expedition into the territory of the Louisiana Purchase with William Clark. It was 55 feet long with an eight-foot beam and could carry 12 tons of cargo while drawing as little as two feet of water. It was equipped so that it could be sailed, rowed, poled or towed from the shoreline.

The flatboat is a river craft of another description and profile. Rectangular, flat-bottomed and fitted with boarded-up sides that range up to 3 feet in height, it resembles a sturdy tub with a hull that displaces water and thus floats in the river, making it different from a raft that floats on the water. Because it is designed as a one-way vessel, destined to be broken-up for lumber upon reaching its downstream destination, it is different from a keelboat that can be maneuvered both down and up a river. Constructed of planks of green oak lumber fastened with wooden pins to heavier frames of timber, the flatboat was not restricted to any standard size. Commonly no more 20 feet wide, length could range in excess of 100 feet. The larger versions had a shelter for farm animals on the stern and a forward cabin for passengers plus a cooking area. Propelling these simple craft required skill and agility. Side-mounted "sweeps" were used for moving the craft into the current and for pulling into slack water, rather than for propulsion. A rudder and a short "gouger" oar on the bow allowed for additional maneuverability.

Flatboats first appeared on the Ohio River in the early 1780s. Most of them had been constructed by unskilled farmers with limited tools, to transport a variety of goods down river as far as New Orleans. The cargo varied with the individual harvest of the farm: corn, wheat, tobacco, whiskey, lumber, potatoes, cotton, chickens, cattle and pigs. Throughout the years prior to the initiation of the Civil War they were a common sight on the Ohio and Mississippi Rivers. Between 1810 and 1820 an average of 3,000 flatboats annually descended the Ohio River, but by 1857 only 540 were docked in New Orleans, down from some 2,800 ten years prior.

History records that General Josiah Harmar, senior officer in the American Army from 1784 to 1791, ordered an inventory of the number of flatboats descending the Ohio River during a seven-month period in the winter of 1786-1787. The resulting report indicated the passage of 127 boats, carrying 2,689 people, 1,333 horses, 756 cattle and 102 wagons. This rising tide of flatboat traffic soon began to invade the major tributaries of the Ohio.

The Great Miami River is some 170 miles in length, drains an area of 5,400 square miles and flows from its origin upstream from Indian Lake south and southwest to its confluence with the Ohio River west of Cincinnati. When discussing the history of early shipping on this river, it is important to know just how far upstream a hand-propelled boat can navigate, a process defined as traveling over water in a boat or ship. This question, relevant to the Great Miami River, was argued before the U. S. Court of Appeals, Sixth Circuit, when the U. S. Army Corps of Engineers sought extended jurisdiction over those sections of the river that were legally and operationally "navigable." The opposing party, the Miami Valley Conservancy District, agreed the river was passable up to the city of Cincinnati, but questioned the degree of navigability

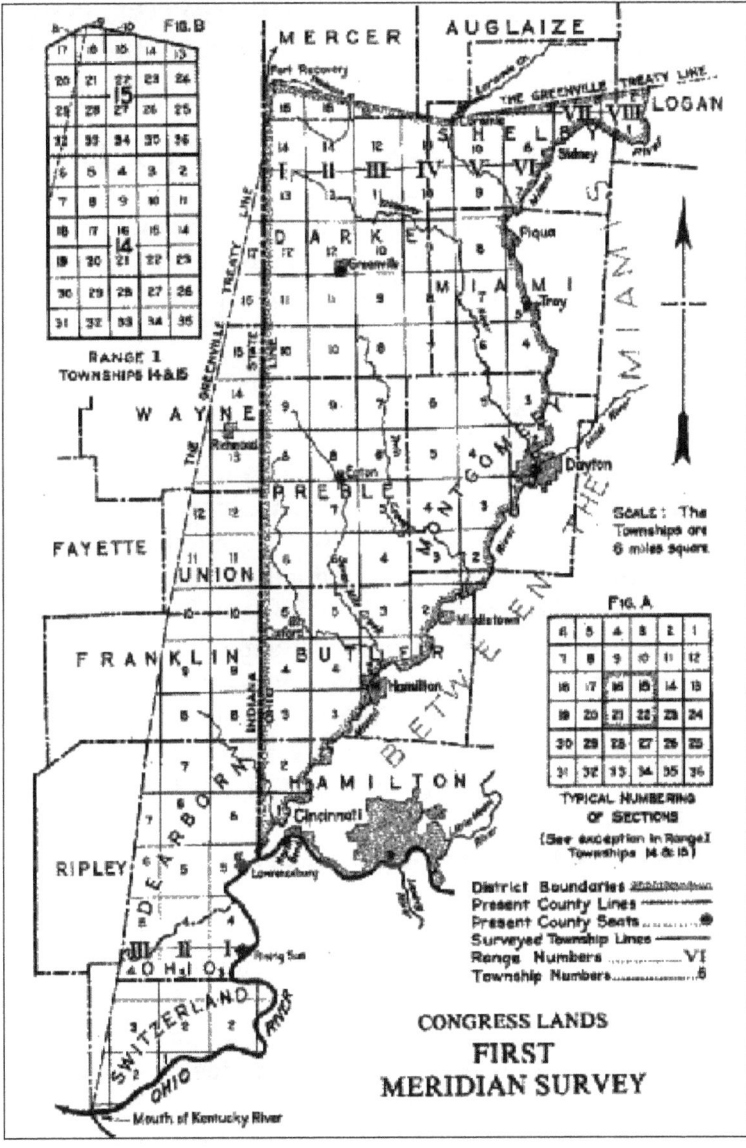

First Meridian Survey conducted between the years 1798 and 1801. Territory mapped includes lands lying between the Great Miami River and the Ohio-Indiana border.

up to Mile 117, near Piqua and then beyond to Mile 153.5, above Sidney, as well as that of Loramie Creek from its mouth to Mile 21, above the rural community of Fort Loramie.

Argued on May 20, 1982 and decided on November 12 the same year, the final wording of case 692 F2d 447 was determined on the basis of historical data, a review of which is not only interesting to any student of early river traffic, but is most pertinent when considering the movement of river craft through Shelby County during the years prior to the Civil War:

"The Corp's determination of navigability of . . . the Great Miami River from Mile 117 to Mile 153.5 rests on early military expeditions. In the late Eighteenth Century military expeditions transported supplies up the rivers to several forts in southwestern Ohio. As many as thirty-two men could have been required to pull a loaded flatboat upstream. Military use of the rivers through great quantities of manpower was not the customary mode of travel for settlers and farmers of the time. This use of the rivers by military expeditions does not prove the susceptibility of use for interstate commerce . . . (therefore) the tributaries of the River and the River from Mile 117 to Mile 153.5 are not navigable . . . Without specific evidence of successful commercial navigation on the Loramie Creek, by keelboat or otherwise, we cannot find that the Creek was used as a highway for interstate commerce. The Loramie Creek is not a navigable waterway of the United States."

The historic record, however, casts a shadowy degree of doubt on the findings of this case. According to information gathered by Walter Havighurst, Regents Professor of English Emeritus, Miami University, David Lowry of Dayton loaded, in the winter of 1799, his recently constructed flatboat with barrels of grain, numerous pelts and some 500 well-cured venison hams. When the water level rose in the spring, he cast off and two months later docked in New Orleans, where he sold the cargo and boat and returned to Ohio by horseback. This is the very first recorded flatboat trip to New Orleans via the Great Miami, Ohio and Mississippi River route, but others soon followed. Records show flatboats arrived in New Orleans from the Great Miami River each year from 1800 until 1830 and that as many as 79 to 130 were sighted on the river during the several spring months that form the high-water period of any given year. They averaged 70 long by 20 feet wide and drew 3 feet of water when fully loaded.

According to Professor Havighurst, boat travel upstream from Dayton was at the time also possible. Over the winter months of 1809-1810, a river cargo line was organized by Henry Desbrow and Paul Butler, with the intention of operating from Dayton to Lake Erie. These partners built two keelboats in a small shipyard located near the Dayton courthouse and moved them along Main Street on log rollers to the river edge. The boats were then floated up the Great Miami River to the mouth of Loramie Creek -- a point 0.7 miles south of what is today the dividing line between Shelby and Miami counties -- with the hope of using the waters of the Loramie to navigate further, but soon they were stopped by shallow water. One boat was then pulled overland through Shelby County and across a 12-mile-long portage to the St. Marys River, where it was employed to move cargo downstream to Lake Erie via the Auglaize and Maumee Rivers. The other boat carried cargo back and forth along the Great Miami River. This operation was most certainly successful, for in 1819 a second line of keelboats began to transport material up the Miami to Toledo via the Loramie portage.

This account is evidence that while keelboats were employed at one time, and perhaps only for brief periods of time, to transport cargo from Dayton to Lake Erie, their passage through Shelby County was by a means that is best described as "overland," rather than "over water."

During these early years, river traffic was sporadic and limited to periods of seasonal high water. A case in point occurred in 1819 when a large, 70-foot long keelboat arrived in Dayton from Cincinnati carrying 12 tons of cargo. This was the singular keelboat that had been maneuvered upstream in a number of years, the result of low water and river obstruction caused by sand bars and manmade fish traps. Other periods of unusual activity were reported: in 1825, a fleet of more than 30 boats, gathered in and from points upstream to Dayton, cast off bound for New Orleans carrying quantities of flour, pork and whiskey and two years later a dozen boats successfully made the same journey carrying the same list of material.

A high water mark in river traffic had been reached however, for in

February of 1828 the last boat left Dayton bound for the port of New Orleans. Within a matter of months shipments south were being consigned to packet boats traveling along the segment of the Miami-Eire Canal that had just been opened to Dayton. Riverboat travel to the north, however, continued until 1837 when the canal was completed to Piqua.

The general historical account of river cargo traveling from Cincinnati to Toledo is not clear on just how far upstream the Loramie Creek was navigable, especially during periods of heavy river flow. An answer might be found in an article in *The Sidney Journal* issue of April 24, 1891, discussing a drowning that had taken place in Loramie Creek in Van Buren Township, northeast of Fort Loramie. The account states "at the point where the accident occurred the stream is not more than three or four feet deep, and probably about 20 feet wide." Certainly, the waters of Loramie Creek were sufficient enough to take the life of a five-year-old boy, but were they of the volume necessary to float a small, lightly-loaded keelboat upstream?

The history of flatboat and keelboat travel along the Ohio River and its principal tributaries lasted but some three decades, but during that time this mode of entrepreneurial transportation gave opportunity to many rural families to broaden their vistas and trade their agricultural harvests for a wide variety of industrial products that greatly enhanced their lives. This era came to an end, not because it was not successful, but because the eras of canal and railroad transportation were more successful.

PROGRESSIVE UNION PROSPECTS

It was quite a lengthy sentence, and it was most certainly not couched in words meant to sooth the delicate of spirit, but then if it had been written in language both soothing and socially correct William Binkley, the editor of *The Sidney Journal*, probably would not have bothered to publish it at all. Attributed to the Honorable B. G. Northrop, it was part of a much longer article titled "Village Improvement and Tree Planting" that ran in the April issue of the American Agriculturist:

> Our best towns, without an improvement society, often fall far short of what they might be and ought to be, for in them, here and there, are found neglected private grounds, dilapidated dwellings, barns and sheds, or a street fronting the house ugly with piles of decaying brush, or chips, old cans, harrows, carts or sleds, a fence with missing pickets, or a disabled gate, which gives an air of shiftlessness, sadly marring the effect of an otherwise beautiful village.

Thus began the rallying call to a lecture scheduled for the evening of April 25, 1892, in Monumental Hall. Mr. Northrop didn't come cheap -- his speaking fee was $60 -- but the cost had already been raised by private subscription and the presentation would therefore be "free to the public."

The timing was more than coincidental, for just the previous Monday the agenda of the regular meeting of the City Council contained several items of related interest: property owners along Clay Street, between Miami and Main avenues, wanted a grade for gutters; a resolution ordering sidewalks along Miami and West avenues was read; and Councilman Gartley reminded everyone of the unsightly jogs that marred many city streets.

For years, merchants, community leaders and citizen groups had been saying the time had come to take action. Throughout the city gravel roads gave way to dust with the passage of every horse and carriage and barren, desolate landscapes that could become areas of beauty with the planting of just a few dollars worth of shrubs were commonplace. *The Journal* summarized the situation in words both hopeful and optimistic, "Sidney, it is pleasant to state, is alive and growing and perfectly conscious of the fact . . . not as some towns are, like the Irishman's mud-turtle -- dead, but not aware of it."

If the brevity of the newspaper review is any indication, the attendance at the free village improvement lecture was, as is said, "nothing to really write home about." It seems Mr. Northrop "treated in a general way the benefits of improvement, and made a few practical suggestions in horticulture -- the planting of the English larch tree and Japanese ivy was recommended -- (but) it is believed some in the audience were disappointed in not hearing more suggestions in detail." Reading between the lines might perhaps indicate Northrop's speaking fee was perhaps excessive:

> To have told an intelligent looking audience what every intelligent person should know would have been to presume more upon the ignorance of his listeners than a shrewd lecturer is willing to do; hence, matters relating to width of sidewalks, depth of gutters, removal of trash from streets, etc. were not touched upon.

The evening was, however, not a total loss. Prior to the lecture, "Staley's orchestra rendered one of its finest overtures, greatly to the entertainment of the audience," and following the presentation W. A.

Graham, chairman of the meeting, entertained a motion to organize an improvement society. As quickly as approval was given, S. J. Hatfield, Frank Hunter and F. A. Rowley were asked to draft a constitution.

Less than two weeks later, at a public meeting held in the assembly room of the courthouse, the gathered citizens voted unanimously for formation of the Sidney Progressive Union, and an Executive Committee was formed, composed of five officers and an advisory group of "five ladies and five gentlemen."

Hope sprang anew that a dingy Sidney might soon be transformed into a radiant Sidney through a process designed, in the words of *The Journal*, "not to agitate the expenditure of public funds, but rather to encourage private enterprise and pride of home surroundings." An operating budget was to be raised by an initiation fee of 25 cents and annual dues of $1.00, or life membership for a one-time, one-sum payment of $25.00.

Over the course of the next six months the leaders began a firestorm of activities, fueled by the general agreement that "the Union now has hold of the right horn of the dilemma, and can and will accomplish a great deal of good." Successes, however, came slowly, some of significant magnitude, some of intermittent value and others of passing interest:

> ---Frank Hunter was charged with obtaining the consent of the City Commissioners to allow the planting of flowerbeds in the courthouse square. The women members of the Executive Committee were authorized to execute the approved plan.

> ---Mmes. B. Slusser, E. H. Arbuckle, W. O. Amann and Jacob Piper were appointed to seek, and obtain, an appropriation for the construction of ornamental water fountains at the four corners of the public square. Two months later the ladies happily announced the City Commissioners were indeed willing "to have four fountains erected in the courthouse square at a cost of $350 to $400 apiece."

> ---W. A. Graham reported his committee had successfully reached an agreement with city officials allowing the placement of watering troughs on "North and South Main Avenue at its junctions with

Ohio Avenue, on the Hardin Hill and on Fair Avenue as far out as the water mains reach." The matter of the removal of the three existing horse troughs near the square had been discussed, but such "talk did not crystalize into a motion." The committee was, however, reminded that state laws authorized the trustees of Clinton Township to contribute an annual appropriation of $50 for providing and maintaining public watering facilities.

---E. E. Kah, the jeweler, offered "the prize of an eight day, Ingraham movement, cathedral gong and half hour strike clock, surmounted by a handsome bronze figure," to that property owner who "shall make the greatest general improvement in grounds or premises before August 15." By mid-June the competition for the prize clock was heating up. S. L. Wicoff reported he had torn down his front yard fence and was changing the grade of "his already beautiful lot on North Main Avenue." Hoping his efforts might be the winning bid, E. L. Hoskins announced the removal of his front fence and the sodding of his "lawn out to his splendid cement walk." Chiming in, *The Sidney Journal* added "at least 20 front fences have been taken away in different parts of the town during the past weeks."

When Dr. Edwin LeFevre returned to Sidney from an extended rail trip throughout the eastern and southern portions of the country, he inquired if anything might be done to clean up the appearance of the grounds of the two rail stations located in the city. In response he was appointed to a "special railway committee" charged with opening "correspondence with the officers of the railways passing through Sidney in the hope of getting something done about the stations." Within a matter of weeks a committee had developed a draft petition for submission to the home office of the Cincinnati, Hamilton and Dayton railway in wordage that clearly proposed a "you scratch my back and we will scratch yours in return" approach to the problem:

> The undersigned patrons of your road and residents of Sidney respectively represent that it would be in line with the general spirit of improvement now pervading our town if your road would park the depot grounds and erect a new passenger station at Sidney. To this end we pledge you our hearty cooperation,

and beg leave to express a high appreciation of past and present favors in the way of facilities for travel and shipment furnished us by your road.

Then, the Cleveland, Cincinnati, Chicago and St. Louis Railroad, known to everyone as the Big Four route, requested permission to build a new switching station across North Street. In a challenging response, the Progressive Union Executive Committee suggested approval if, and only if, construction was confined to two acres of easily accessible, publicly owned land in the western limits of the city -- and shade trees be planted around the existing company passenger station.

By the late summer of 1892 the work of the Progressive Union was proceeding in a manner both qualitative and quantitative, with its various committees distributing suggestions and financial largesse throughout the city. The tasks at hand ranged from those of sidewalk and gutter construction to topographical ornamentation, but one particular form of community-wide adornment had caught the collective fancy of homeowners, merchants and city fathers alike -- shade trees.

In a lengthy article published on July 8, *The Sidney Journal* gave advice to green-thumb citizens interested in dressing up their property with choice, tall, woody plants: "The form should be compact and symmetrical and not of a spreading and pendant tendency. . . the foliage should be ample, of early spring verdure, and of rich and varied tints in the fall . . . the branches should be elastic rather than brittle, that they may withstand heavy storms and gales . . . with a hardiness essential to enable it to withstand the attacks of insects and the exigencies of city life." The silver maple and the American elm were recommended as the trees-of-choice for Sidney.

When Mr. H. Haerlin "the well known landscape gardener, under whose direction the work at the Soldier's Home at Sandusky is being carried out, and who has been employed by the State for 30 years in similar work," came to town, the Union Executive Committee gave him two tasks: "make the water works park the loveliest spot in town"and "layout an addition to the cemetery." No sooner had he changed into his field clothes than he was whisked off to a tour of both locations. In the former he quickly envisioned two miniature lakes that could be formed by damning Tilberry Run, the tributary to the Great Miami River that flows along the south border of the water works property. When he and the committee visited next the newly acquired, five-acre addition to Graceland Cemetery, the discussion quickly turned to the development of a carriage drive running "diagonally through the ground . . . in graceful curves to the right and left so as to encircle the property." By Friday afternoon, having been in town for less than 30 hours, Mr. Haerlin had completed his work, and he left town "at once for Chillicothe." The task of beautifying Sidney was moving along at a brisk pace -- or was it?

One year later, in a report of a regular summer meeting of the Progressive Union, *The Sidney Journal* gave notice that progress was not as it supposedly should be: the streets were not clean, horses and cows were running at large, and the planting of shade trees -- or lack thereof -- was still a subject of intense discussion. Given the floor, Dr. Edwin LeFevre vented his frustration in a lengthy monologue directed to both the assembled audience and the community-at-large:

> There has been, I am sorry to say a disposition to make light of the efforts of the Progressive Union. It is said of us that we talk a great deal and accomplish very little. There may be some truth in this, but if all those who scoff at our efforts would have joined hands heartily with us much more light might have been accomplished. There are . . . in every community like this about three grand divisions of society. The first . . . includes those who are actively progressive. They know what should be done, how it should be accomplished and are willing to make any reasonable effort to carry forward any good work or reform. Next in order comes the middle class . . . a majority of the community . . . as a rule able to appreciate the truth . . . and often make spasmodic efforts in the

right direction . . . but their efforts are not well sustained . . . are liable to be influenced by selfish or sinister motives. Lastly, there is the third class . . . the densely ignorant and the notoriously vicious and vile . . . destitute of good impulses . . . who can always be counted on as apposed to every thing which has for its object the advancement of the community or of society.

Catching his breath LeFevre continued in a vein somewhat more encouraging:

I have no doubt Sidney will continue to go forward. There is every reason to hope that the progress during the next 20 years will be even greater . . . Sidney will some day have a system of sewage and a garbage cremator . . . many more beautiful homes, lawns and shade streets . . . new railway stations, new school buildings and may even have a new opera house. Shall we be permitted to behold and enjoy them, or shall they be left for those who shall come after us?

The gauntlet had been flung, the charges made and the exasperation expressed in terms certain and unvarnished. As the weeks, months and years passed, the work of the Progressive Union continued, but at a pace similar to the slow and often halted development of Central Park, the urban greenway Frederick Law Omsted designed for New York City that was built over a 16 year period, 1857-1873.

Nine years after Dr. LeFevre delivered his challenge to the citizens of Sidney, beautification was still a subject of extended debate. In July 1902, for example, the *Sidney Daily News* published a report outlining the advantages and disadvantages of the use of six different types of material -- granite, brick, wood, asphalt, Belgian block and macadam -- used to pave streets throughout America. A concluding challenge, "Whether a town or city lays pavements, depends on whether the property owners are willing to pay for it," only proved that times and sentiment had changed little over the years.

The Progressive Union is now a chapter of local history, its successes and failures all but forgotten and its membership preserved as family names chiseled in graveyard granite, but the desire for community beauty still exists. The choice of Sidney as an "All American City" in 1964 and the peaceful byways and family gathering groves of Tawawa Park provide proof that the spirit, the principles and the animating forces of the Progressive Union live on in the 21st century.

CCC COMPANY 3526

The surnames spoke clearly of the western European origins of many of the residents of Shelby County: Vonderhyde, Henke, Schloss, Huecker and Paulus. There were twelve of them, and while they differed in demeanor and dress they were quite similar in other aspects—aged between 17 and 28, unmarried, in generally good physical condition and jobless. Otherwise, they would have not been accepted. They were all males, for females were not eligible. After the completion of a thorough physical examination, they began a 10-day program of instruction in the rudiments of camp discipline, along with an introduction to the art of making beds and packing equipment. Their instructors emphasized respect for group leaders and the necessity of functioning in a group environment. Within a few short years most would serve in World War II, and then each one would become lifelong representatives of the "Greatest Generation." For the next six months, however, they were members of the Civilian Conservation Corps, better known then and now as the CCC.

When Franklin D. Roosevelt was sworn in as President, he knew he had his work cut out for him. His predecessor, Herbert Hoover, had firmly believed that the depressing economic conditions of that time would somehow disappear without the help of the federal government, if only local and state jurisdictions would address the problem in an effective manner. But 3 1/2 years had passed since that dark day in 1929 when it all began, and unemployment was now at a level of 25 percent. The

American public was weary and disheartened, so as soon as the last of the inaugural parade marchers had disappeared around the corner, the new President began his whirlwind and historic "first 100 days in office." As governor of the State of New York, he had conducted a similar program and thus, on March 21, 1933, his 19th day in office, he addressed Congress:

> I propose to create (a program) to be used in simple work, not interfering with normal employment, and confining itself to forestry, the prevention of soil erosion, flood control and similar projects...of definite, practical value...as a means of creating future national wealth.

The Emergency Conservation Work Act was presented to Congress the very same day, approved by voice vote ten days later, and on April 5th Roosevelt issued Executive Order 6101, establishing the Civilian Conservation Corps. The order stipulated that the program, soon jovially referred to as Roosevelt's Tree Army, be administered jointly by four federal departments: Labor, charged with recruitment; War, given the responsibility of operating the camps; Agriculture, organized the work projects; and Interior, in charge of supervising the projects. The very first enrollee was selected on April 8th, and nine days later the first camp, NF-1, was platted in George Washington National Forest, outside Luray, Virginia.

By early July some 250,000 young men were being assigned to more than 1,460 camps located throughout the country. It took 14 weeks, from proposal to full operation, to establish a program that would peak in enrollment in 1935 and ultimately involve more than three million young men.

The *Sidney Daily News* announcement appeared next to that of the grand opening of the Rhees Clothes Shop in the storefront formerly occupied by the Kraft Shoe Store, on the north side of the public square. The men's clothing store was to stay in operation far longer, but the approval of a CCC camp for Shelby County was undoubtedly the more important news of that day of April 15, 1935. Congress had recently passed a colossal $4.8 billion work relief bill, and a portion of the money was to be used locally to support 60 enrollees in "conservation work (intended) to build men as well as grow trees." Obviously this was welcome news, but it did stir a bit of controversy, since the news article emphasized enrollment was wholly voluntary; "no coercion or pressure is used…no one is being 'drafted' or 'conscripted' for this work." Interested individuals were urged to file their applications at the Shelby Country Relief Board office in the Ohio Building.

A campsite was soon identified "on property just north of the corporation line on the east side of the Dixie highway in what is known as the Parkwood addition." True to the wording of the federal legislation, Captain C. T. Williams, formerly associated with the 379th U. S. Army Engineers, arrived in Sidney in July with a staff of two officers and 23 men with orders to oversee the work of establishing headquarters and approving plans for water, sanitary sewer and electric light arrangements for "Camp Sidney," officially designated as CCC Company 3526, Drainage Camp Number 5. Knowing the value of positive publicity, Williams wasted no time in announcing the camp would be built to accommodate 200 young men, rather than 60 as originally reported; necessary equipment and supplies would be purchased through local businesses; and all work details handled through local contractors. The community considered this announcement a win-win situation for everyone.

The first contingent of 140 boys came to town on the 2:00 PM, Baltimore and Ohio train from Cincinnati, where they had been assembled from several southern Ohio counties. Because recruitment was taking place simultaneously with camp construction, regulation army tents were used to temporarily house the enrollees. The young men received blankets, sheets, pillows and pillow cases, denim dungarees, coats and hats, mess kits, shoes and other items of equipment, and before anyone had any time to check out the lay of the land they received orders to begin digging ditches in which to lay a 300-foot, 6-inch water main as well as a 2,500-foot, 6-inch sanitary sewer pipe for the camp. A new way of life had begun, one affiliated with organization and cooperation directed toward the group rather than the individual. A five-day-a-week regime began with reveille at 6:00 followed by breakfast and assignment of the day's work, starting at 7:30 o'clock. After a one-hour lunch break, work continued until 3:30, but then the remainder of the day was free for individual activities: baseball, volleyball, tennis or perhaps the writing of a letter home to the family.

At his presentation before the Rotary Club, the commanding officer of Camp Sidney explained that one of the principal purposes of the CCC organization was "to aid in the social development of the nation, take the boys off the streets and remove the chance for criminal tendencies to develop because of idle hands." Each enrollee earned $30 per month, but $25 of that went directly to the family, leaving $5 for personal expenditures. Lest this seem a bit harsh to the assembled Rotarians, the guest speaker was quick to state that because the "CCC is a relief measure, the return of allotment money to men in camp would defeat its purpose."

The next order of business was deciding what type of work would be conducted at the local facility. In other states and regions, the assignments constituted a diverse list: creating fire towers, planting trees, protecting wildlife habitats, inventorying timber stands and constructing campgrounds, picnic shelters, swimming pools, fireplaces and restrooms in national parks. Because these assignments were not relevant to the farmlands of Shelby County, the U. S. Bureau of Agriculture Engineering stepped forward and announced Camp Sidney would become one of 46 camps assigned to construct and improve drainage systems designed to control erosion processes during times of flooding. By August, federal officials were working with the county commissioners, County Agriculture Agent R. W. Munger and the county surveyor to determine an extended list of public ditches that needed to be cleaned, widened and rip-rapped.

By mid-decade the national CCC organization was operating at full force and supposedly full efficiency, but by today's standards conditions were not always ideal. In a technical sense discrimination was not permitted, but in reality Blacks and other minority groups faced numerous difficulties. Pressed for an explanation, Robert Fechner, a former union vice president President Roosevelt personally chose to be the National Director of the CCC, explained rather weakly that there was a "complete segregation of colored and white enrollees (but) segregation is not discrimination." Eventually, some 250,000 African-Americans had been enrolled in 150 all-black CCC companies. More than 80,000 Native Americans ironically worked to reclaim the

US Army personnel training CCC recruits.

lands that had once been theirs for untold generations. The CCC concept was indeed flawed, but overall it was considered to be one of the most successful of all the New Deal programs established by the Roosevelt administration to help America claw its way out of the Great Depression.

As the warm temperatures of summer began to evolve to the cool breezes of autumn, Camp Sidney assumed an atmosphere of identity. A recreational field had been laid out, complete with baseball diamonds, tennis courts and horseshoe pits. The boys were still living in army tents, but 13 carloads were scheduled to arrive with equipment and supplies – worth a whopping $17,000 -- necessary for the construction of 16 buildings. There were blueprints for four barracks, one mess hall, a recreation hall, quarters for technical services, technical supply rooms, garage, tool room, headquarters, officers quarters, shower rooms, store room, infirmary and perhaps the most important facility of all – the latrine. When Judge Charles M. Wyman, on behalf of the local Kiwanis Club, officiated over the presentation of a flagpole and the American flag was raised for the first time on November 11, Camp Sidney was declared officially open.

With surveys completed and lists of requested projects finalized and approved, the boys of Company 3526 – now numbering in excess of 220 individuals – received their assignments. The work could not be classed as glamorous and exciting but after a week or two of laboring in the hot sun with shovel and hoe, most participants could agree on one point – the regimen did build both muscle and appetite. The typical CCC youth enlisted at the age of 18 years and worked in the program for nine months. During that time he gained anywhere from 12 to 30 pounds in weight and a good one-half inch in height. Since the great majority could boast of only an eighth grade education, vocational training programs would ultimately involve more than 90 percent of the enrollees. While most of the work was labor intensive, some was death defying. Forty-seven were killed in the process of fighting forest fires and 300 died in 1935 when a hurricane swept through three camps in southern Florida.

After nine months of operation, Camp Sidney was opened to the general public during a "special get-together" organized to allow the camp personnel to show appreciation for the community's continued support and good will. Apparently such support was never in doubt, especially when it was announced that each month anywhere from $2,500 to $3,500 was being spent on the purchase of camp food alone. And, a similar amount was paid in wages to camp officers and technical support personnel, much of which was "spent locally for theatre, candy, ice cream, cigars, cigarettes, civilian wearing apparel, shoes and haircuts." Work had been completed on seven projects and two more – involving the elimination of silt and debris accumulation along Mile Creek and Loramie Creek – were to be finalized as soon as outdoor working conditions improved. To date, more than 13,000 enrollee man hours had been extended in improving the degree of drainage relief to local farmers by repairing farm tile laterals, protecting washed banks from further erosion and building headwalls for drain outlets. The rural segment of the population was especially appreciative when farmland specifics were outlined -- the removal of 620,000 square yards of brush and water-loving shrubs whose root growth caused the clogging of tile drains and the choking of drainage ditches and the excavation of 16,800 cubic yards of earth and silt through labor conservatively estimated to have a value of $100,000. With success such as this, it was no wonder that Camp Sidney was awarded the Findlay Sector Pennant for the "most outstanding camp for the month of May, 1936."

By mid-decade, the national CCC program was beginning to peak in both popularity and federal support. Improved business conditions and the formation of distant and threatening war clouds caused hearts and minds to focus on new developments. A rumor began to be circulated around the public square that Camp Sidney, along with 700 other camps nationwide, would be discontinued, but protests by a bloc of Democratic congressmen effectively squelched such thoughts. The year 1939, however, brought about a major change when Congress, through authorization of the Federal Security Agency, consolidated several offices under one director and CCC lost its status as an independent organization. Finally, in 1942, Congress authorized federal funding to close all remaining camps, but the CCC program was never officially terminated. With the reallocation of existing equipment and structures, it became a useful model for a variety of conservation programs that were developed following the end of World War II. Today, more than 100 CCC-related work-project programs exist in some 40 states, involving youth and young adults in community service, training and educational activities.

Franklin D. Roosevelt said it quite well when he addressed the nation on the occasion of the third anniversary of the Civilian Conservation Corps in 1936:

> Records show that the results achieved in the protection and improvement of our timbered domain, in the arrest of soil wastage, in the development of needed recreational areas, in wild life conservation and in flood control have been as impressive as the results achieved in the rehabilitation of youth. It has been demonstrated that young men can be put to work in our forests, parks, and fields on projects which benefit both the nation's youth and conservation generally.

If it were possible for them to be assembled today for one last roll call, it surely would be safe to say the boys and young men of Company 3526, Drainage Camp Number 5 – also known as Camp Sidney – would be in complete agreement with this presidential statement.

LIGHT UP TIME

Life on a farm during the early decades of the 20th century most certainly had its ups and downs. Many a senior citizen who grew up in rural Shelby County during that time had a tendency to look back in nostalgia and view it as "the good old days." But then, with a little reflection, thoughts might stray to patterns of daily life, and the old ways, all of a sudden, could take on an aura of fatigue and repetition. When described in detail, the processes of merely starting the morning and completing the evening are today unimaginable to anyone younger than 70 years of age. And then, there was that cycle of life that extended from Sunday through Saturday, and the experienced person could become tired with reflection.

Long before the sun appeared along the distant edge of the cornfield, the cows had to be milked, by hand and under the dim light of a kerosene lantern that hung from a nearby post and cast a huge shadow along the floor, making it quite difficult to see just where the operation was taking place. Move the lantern closer to the work at hand, and one ran the risk of a fire.

The next task was to gather more hay from the loft and stomp up and down on it so it would be soft enough for the cows to eat. If one had a few extra minutes, there was always the need to stick several dozen ears into the corn sheller and build up the supply of feed for the other animals. In all, it was tedious work even if one were proficient and able to milk ten animals every 60 minutes. Whatever one's ability, and however many animals, it was best to leave the barn before daybreak, for daylight meant the start of fieldwork.

Ideally during these early hours another member of the family was gathering wood from the stacked pile located outdoors and stirring the nighttime embers in the cook stove into life. Then, water had to be gathered. If the house had been built over a cistern kept full by rainwater running off the roof, then only hand pumping was required. If not, then a bucket had to be cranked down the well, not once but multiple times. In the worst case, a trip was made to the nearby creek with a wheel barrow containing two empty milk cans.

Monday was washday, probably all day. Whatever family members were responsible heated water on the wood stove and poured it into a tub on the porch, along with the dirty clothes. The removal of dirt required paddle agitation and frequent use of a rippled washboard and hand-made lye soap. Following a rinsing in a second tub of water, each item was hung on a clothesline and left to dry in the sunshine and fresh air. Tuesday meant ironing, using two or more six-pound implements made -- naturally -- of iron with a handle and heavy flat bottom. While one was being heated on the stove, the other was in use until it became cold and then a transfer was made.

Saturday was bath day. During the warm months bathing could take place in the creek, but during the cold season a big, body-sized, galvanized washtub filled with hot water occupied the kitchen floor and the task was quickly completed regardless of anyone's sense of modesty. Refrigeration of food such as meat, butter and milk was accomplished in a cold storage room dug into a hillside or, lacking such topography, by wrapping wet burlap sacks around a cooler that was kept in the shade.

In better equipped rural homes a periodically activated gas generator charged a series of batteries used to power a primitive light system for a week or to operate a radio tuned into the daily news and the Saturday night Grand Ole Opry show beamed out of Nashville, Tennessee. An alternative process produced light formed by the burning of a gas created by the immersion of calcium carbide pellets in a tank of water.

Such was daily life in the great majority of American rural homes, even as recently as the mid-1930s when a mere 10% of farm families were hooked up to so-called central-station electrical service. In contrast, other countries had already achieved considerable progress in supplying electricity to rural households: Germany 90%, France 95% and the Netherlands 100%.

Rural Electrification Administration Poster

By 1935, privately owned utility companies controlled more than 90% of the electric-power industry in the United States. Feasibility studies of the problems and benefits of extending service to the farming community suggested the typical farmer would not use enough power to justify the costs of service. From a business point of view, the electric power industry had minimal interest in the rural market. The 1934 report by the Mississippi Valley Committee, a federal advisory group appointed by President Franklyn D. Roosevelt, stressed however:

> Unless the Federal Government assumes an active leadership, assisted... by State and local agencies, only a negligible part of this task (of supplying electricity to rural areas) can be accomplished within any reasonable time.

At the time, it was estimated that if the rate of progress of the degree of rural electrification accomplished over the period 1924-1933 were extended for the next half century, only 50% of American farm homes would be electrified. Clearly, and in spite of its being the fifth year of the Great Depression, something had to be done.

As measured against any standard of the 20th century, it was the worst of times. America was experiencing one of those definable and critical moments that differentiate the passage of time into distinct periods. Historians would have to regress decades, to the Civil War, to find a crisis that affected as much of the country and its people. Years later, when John Maynard Keynes, the noted British economist, was asked if there had ever been a comparable period, he replied: "Yes, it was called the Dark Ages, and it lasted 400 years."

Over the four-year period that separated the time of the height of prosperity in America, in the late 1920s, to the depths of the Depression, in 1933, economic factors drastically declined: consumer prices and expenditures by 18 percent, the gross national product by 29 percent, construction by 78 percent, the Dow Jones Industrial Average by 83 percent and investments by 98 percent. Only unemployment rose, from 3 percent to 25 percent of the working population.

The mood of the American public suffered accordingly, creating national feelings ranging from despair to near anarchy. Some people prepared by hoarding canned foods in home cellars modified so they could survive any future siege. Others undertook more drastic action, as evidenced by the nighttime looting of broken store windows in Detroit and the use of firearms in Arkansas to force Red Cross officials to increase the pace of emergency food distribution.

While life beyond the limits of the city was equally difficult, the distinguishing factors in rural regions were different. The farm family typically had its garden in season and could rely on home-canned food during the winter and, of course, slaughter a hog as needed, but life hadn't really evolved much since the era of the cave man -- productivity on a daily basis was still largely dependent on the presence of sunlight.

Slowly planners recognized that the extension of electricity to rural areas would not only raise the standard of living and promote a greater sense of economic stability within the agricultural community, but just might be a positive influence on the problem of the migration of youth to urban centers.

Rural electrification at the time, of course, was possible, but the farmer had to pay for the cost of the distribution line, transfer title of the involved property to the utility company and then guarantee the payment of high minimum charges over an extended period of time. Only large farms could justify the expenditure and in the 1930s the typical American farm was not "large." In short, the typical small acreage farmer needed help of the kind that was possible only through organization on a national level.

In his address to Congress in 1935, President Franklyn D. Roosevelt recommended legislation he hoped would reduce the number of unemployed Americans and cited the recommendations of the National Resources Planning Board, a federal panel charged with land and water resource planning and associated public works, as a guide for applicable public expenditures. Recognizing the value of this request Congress included rural electrification as the type of project intended in its passage of the Emergency Relief Appropriation Act of 1935. With this authority, Roosevelt established the Rural Electrification Administration as a temporary agency "to initiate, formulate, administer and supervise a program of approved projects with respect to the generation, transmission and distribution of electric energy in rural areas."

Within a matter of months a new type of organization began to emerge in districts across America -- the "cooperative," an association of independent farmers working with the federal government for the purpose of the construction and operation of rural electric-distribution systems. It was no surprise, therefore, when the *Sidney Daily News* announced in its November 6 issue:

> The Rural Electrification Administration in Washington today approved a 20 year, three percent $350,000 loan to the Shelby County Rural Electric Cooperative, Inc. for the construction of 270 miles of line to serve 1,005 farms.

Today, during the ceremonial digging of the first shovel load of soil on any important project the assembled VIPs, both men and women, are photographed wearing hard hats, preferably chrome plated. On November 11, 1935, however, the scene was different. Every male member of the crowd of community leaders wore a fedora, a soft, brimmed, felt hat that was then the head-cover-of-choice for men, whether their occupation took them to the office or the field. The venue was the municipal electric power plant in Piqua, and the agenda consisted of but one simple task -- the digging of a hole deep enough to hold a typical 40-foot-tall, creosote-treated, southern yellow pine wooden pole upright for a very long time.

National history was in the making when at precisely 10 AM each man turned over, in unison, a clump of dirt marking the beginning of the construction of "the first farmer-owned cooperative electric line in the United States . . . financed by the $100,000,000 federal fund allocated to rural electrification." When the last pole was planted, which according to plan should have been accomplished by April 1 of 1936, and strung with line, farmers from both Miami and Shelby counties would be on-line to "the first undertaking of its kind in the country."

Among the assembled officials was W. R. Joslin, president of the Shelby County Rural Electrification Corporation. When questioned, he explained how the completed power line would run east around the city of Piqua and north into Shelby County, where it would be extended into all sections of the county, leaving no farm or rural family in the dark. Almost immediately, farmers began to hire electricians to wire their homes and barns. When that task was completed, the women of each household were encouraged to consider the purchase of an electric toaster and radio -- and perhaps even an electric vacuum cleaner -- through the Sears Roebuck catalogue.

When the family's home was "hooked up to juice," everyone could sit back and for the first time experience darkness on a voluntary basis. The natural illumination of daylight hours could now be extended into the realm of nighttime obscurity. County Commissioner Henry J. Simon, of Russia, was reported to be the first in line to wire his house.

By the first of the year, various items of construction material were on order, surveyors were staking the line routes, electricians were installing home meters and switch boxes and potential customers were encouraged to sign up for service at the cooperative office located on Wilkinson Avenue. Soon after the last firecracker had lit the sky and the

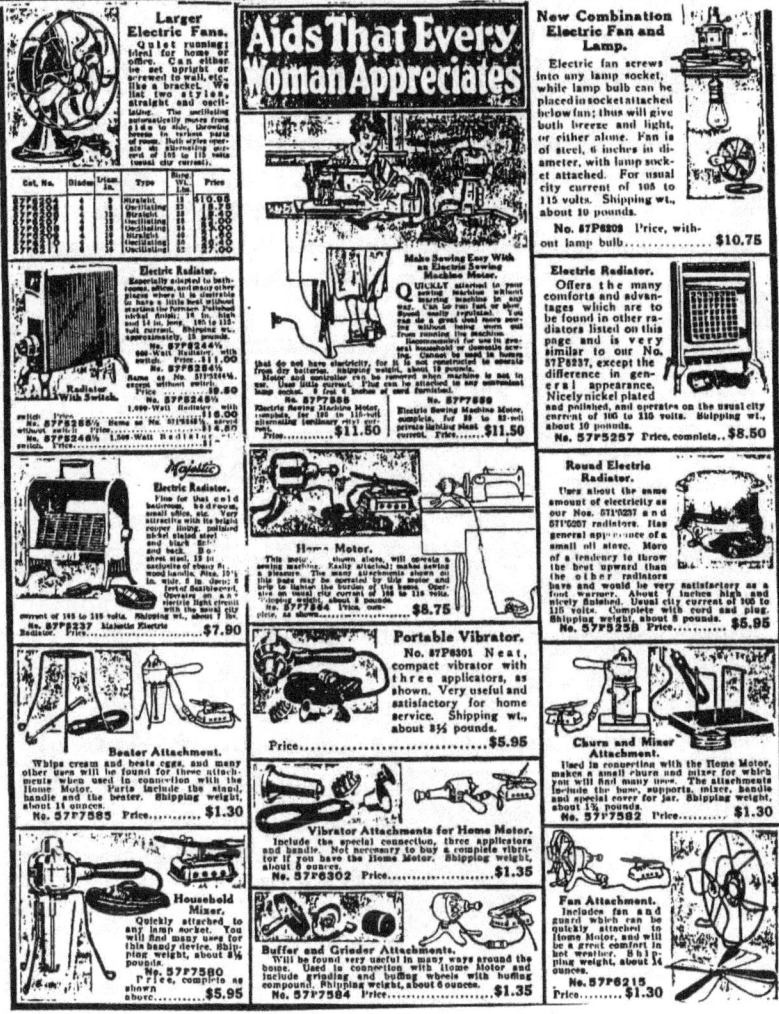

last sparkler had sputtered to silence in celebration of Independence Day, planners were anticipating a day of illumination like none other that had ever occurred in the upper Miami River Valley. The big to-do would take place at the home of Harry Lindsay of Washington Township as soon as possible after sundown, a time selected so as to create the maximum impression upon the expected large crowd.

Finally the moment came -- its takes a long time for darkness to descend in July -- the designated official threw the switch, and the assembly of mostly farmers stood in awe as the six-room farm home was illuminated from "top to bottom and also the barnyard and lane." When the principal speaker, M. D. Lincoln, executive secretary of the Ohio Farm Bureau, concluded his thoughts with the observation he had "yet found a farmer who didn't know what to do with his leisure time when he got some," he perhaps had in mind a related thought. Extra time could be used to generate extra income to be used for the purchase of appliances and the improvement of the economy. After all, these two advantages were really behind the recommendation and creation of the Rural Electrification Administration in the first place. The festivities continued into the night with music furnished by a four-man orchestra, the showing of a short movie and the opening of an open-air tent in which numerous electrical appliances were on display, courtesy of the merchants of downtown Sidney.

In this second decade of the 21st century, America is undergoing yet another revolution, one dependent upon satellite rather than land-line control. For the first time, a generation is living with iPods, smartphones and other miscellaneous hand-held devices, all lacking any type of electrical umbilical cord. It's an amazing time to be alive, but I'll bet if we could be transformed back in time, we would find present-day renovations are nothing compared to that magical time in mid-July of 1936 when luminous, radiant, white, bright light changed life forever for the rural residents of Shelby County

WINGS AND WHEELS

❖ ❖ ❖

The analysis of any catalogue of facts or events requires perspective to determine what has lasting importance. The year of 1938 is a case in point. Around the public square in Sidney, it wasn't a gee-whiz or a gosh-almighty period of time in the minds of many individuals, nor was it one that had any great chance of being tagged as unusually significant. To those in the know, however, it was an important year -- one in transition. The indications are in general unrelated and geographically scattered, but in combination they have their own story to tell.

In America the Dow Jones Industrial Average plunged in midyear to 98.95 after having advanced 153 points from its 1933 Great Depression low of 41.22. Up in New England the Yankee Clipper, a storm of such ferocity it was eclipsed in landfall intensity only by the Great Colonial Hurricane of 1635, killed as many as 800 persons and caused $4.7 billion of damage, as measured in 2013 currency.

And do not forget the night of June 24th. For persons who believed in the relationship of extra-terrestrial events to earthly phenomena, the year surely was memorable. Twelve miles above Chicora, a borough in Butler County, Pennsylvania, a 450-ton meteorite exploded with such destructive power "if it had landed on Pittsburgh there would have been few survivors."

Across a swath of Europe, from Vienna to London, huge blood-red streamers of light emblazoned the northern sky. Scientists at the University of Grenoble reported it was the most intense display of an aurora borealis since 1709. A few devotees of the art form known as "the comics" proclaimed this manifestation of high-altitude electrical disturbance gave impetus a few months later to the creation of Superman, the Man of Steel born on the planet Krypton and rocketed to Earth in the guise of Clark Kent for the purpose of fighting for social justice and against tyranny. Who but this first of a long line of super-heroes had the ability to fight and control a celestial spectacle of such brilliance and color as to have caused otherwise common-sense observers to shout from window-sills all along the Boulevard de la Madeleine: "Paris is on fire."

No sooner had this celestial conflagration been snuffed out in the hearts and minds of the locals than it was reborn in the form of a 62-minute episode aired over the Columbia Broadcasting System in late October. In this radio version of the classic story by H. G. Wells titled "The War of the Worlds," an alien invasion of Earth created near-panic reactions across the United States as listeners fled their homes and banded together in fear of running into "tentacled, pulsating, barely mobile Martians" around the next street corner.

H. G. Wells

Describing this public phenomenon as prime evidence of the decadence and corrupt condition of democracy, Adolf Hitler, chancellor of Nazi Germany, was at the time enjoying the results of his Anschluss, the enforced occupation and annexation of Austria into the Third Reich. Neville Chamberlain, the prime minister of England, considered this action unacceptable and arranged a meeting with the German fuhrer. After a bit of back-and-forth diplomatic squabbling, signatures were applied to the Munich Agreement allowing Nazi Germany to peacefully take over those portions of Czechoslovakia inhabited by German speakers. Chamberlain returned home, announced his belief the agreement was symbolic of "peace for our time," and advised his constituents to go home and get a nice quiet sleep. Five weeks later, paramilitary forces ransacked synagogues and Jewish-owned businesses throughout Germany and parts of Austria, and 30,000 innocent individuals were arrested and incarcerated in concentration camps. This Kristallnacht, or Night of Broken Glass, another step in a continuing program of economic and political persecution of European Jews, is viewed by historians as the beginning of The Holocaust.

Not every bit of news during the year was on the dark side. After three years of disappointment, exploration geologists made an historic discovery on the morning of March 3 at a remote desert site in Saudi Arabia identified as Dammam Number 1. At a depth of 1,440 meters, the rotating bit at the end of a string of drill-pipe suspended within a Standard Oil of California exploration rig struck oil. This site would eventually become the locale of the largest source of crude oil in the world and thereby alter Middle Eastern political relations with the rest of the world well into the 21st century.

Otto Hahn

To the north a German chemist and pioneer in the fields of radioactivity and radiochemistry sent a manuscript to a scientific journal describing the results of his latest laboratory experiments. When he realized he had forgotten a key statement, he telephoned to ask the editor to add the sentence reading: "some platinum group elements previously observed in irradiated uranium... could in fact be technetium." By this simple act, the new version of the article announced to the world the discovery of nuclear fission and Otto Hahn, the author, is today recognized as the "father of nuclear chemistry." The atomic age had been born.

That was the year of 1938, as viewed on the national and international scene. In retrospect it was a time of great significance, one during which many an event or happening planted a germ that would prove to be of meaningful importance to the annals of history.

In Sidney the hometown paper rolled off the presses in the basement of the East Court facility on a sustaining basis throughout the year, and H. V. Kaltenborn continued to deliver his interpretation of the unfolding events in staccato pronouncements during the evening news program on the radio. Community life seemed little different from the year before. What, then, were the events that made life a little less normal or a little more exciting in Shelby County?

The answer lies in the newspaper records stored in the basement of the Amos Public Library. At their first examination, it would seem the year was composed of a series of happenings that, on an individual basis, were of insignificant and temporary interest. Bundled together they still present little evidence the community, or the life styles of its residents, had been changed to any great extent. In light of subsequently occurring world events a listing is unusually provincial: steeplejacks replaced the Holy Angels church cross broken in a recent windstorm with a new, 350-pound, gold leaf cross; the controlling interests of the Peerless Bread Machinery Corporation exchanged hands; the near-term erection of a municipal building was announced; the high school band initiated a campaign to raise a "mile of pennies"; W. R. Minton opened his "fond dream come true" supermarket on North Main Avenue; Monarch erected a new two-story building on Oak Street; and preliminary steps were taken for the development of a U. S. Super Dixie Highway from the Canadian border to the Gulf of Mexico via Shelby County.

Photo compliments of Shelby County Historical Society

A second perusal of the library records, however, identifies two events that must have been of sustained interest to the average reader for a period of time. Each was the source of repeated items listed in the *Sidney Daily News* and each caught the public eye for more than a day or two. One, of national import, dealt with the subject of wings and the other, of familial interest, involved wheels.

Modern-day historians are already grousing about the fact that handwritten letters delivered by the mail service -- the so called "snail mail" -- are quickly becoming a rare item in everyone's mailbox. At one time, communications written in cursive style and delivered by the U. S. Mail by way of train and truck were the principal means through which ordinary citizens kept up on their social and extended family news. While it might take two or three days to move a letter from Cincinnati to Toledo, better and faster processes of delivery were constantly being tested.

On May 10, 1938, Postmaster William B. Swonger completed plans for the local observation of National Air Mail Week, scheduled to begin five days hence. Intended to better acquaint the public with this modern system of mail delivery, the week was specifically selected to mark the 20th anniversary of the establishment of the first airmail route between New York City and Washington, D. C., a distance of 218 miles. Since that inaugural flight the system had expanded to nearly 63,000 miles. Shelby County was, however, not yet involved.

After inspection of the suitability of the designated ground conditions, Theodore Campbell, Inspector for the Bureau of Air Commerce, announced the first local air mail pickup would be made from "the Graham farm, a mile and a half northwest of Sidney on State Route 54." Anyone planning to use this flight for the dispatch of airmail was advised to deliver letters to the post office by noon on Thursday, each item identified by the newly released bi-colored six-cent airmail stamp.

Leaving Celina an hour late, Donald Flower guided his two-winged plane, manufactured by the Waco Aircraft Company of Troy, due south from Wapakoneta, using as his guide the tracks of the Baltimore and Ohio Railroad. Circling once over the Graham farm field, he made a perfect three-point landing at precisely 2:55 PM, a mere ten minutes behind schedule. One thousand persons cheered while three incoming pouches were removed and three outgoing pouches loaded for distribution to Piqua, Troy and Dayton. The Dayton pouch contained mail destined for delivery to "all parts of the country." Within a matter of hours, the North Ohio Avenue post office had sold the last of its new airmail stamps, and the first official airmail flight from Sidney had become a lasting item of history.

One month later, the subhead in the *Sidney Daily News* announced a "soapbox derby to be held in Sidney." The newspaper, the Shelby Motor Company and the Sidney Kiwanis Club had banded together to sponsor a downhill speed competition involving homemade, gravity-powered, wooden racers, open to "any boy between the ages of 9 and 15." The winner would advance to Akron in August where the national finals were to be conducted. The winner of that race would receive a four- year college scholarship.

The idea of designing, building and piloting motorless derby cars down an incline was conceived in 1933 by Myron Scott, a photographer for the *Dayton Daily News*. During one of his frequent treks about town, he observed several boys involved in just such a contest. Intrigued, he invited the youths, along with any of their friends, to gather a week later for a more organized race. To his surprise 19 contestants showed up. Recognizing a promotional opportunity when he saw it, Myron convinced his editor to sponsor such a race and even arranged for cash prizes totaling $200.

On August 19, 362 backyard- and garage-designed cars, constructed of fruit crates and scrap wood and mounted on baby buggy wheels and roller skates, were registered for the inaugural event. The Dayton police department estimated a crowd of 40,000 spectators gathered along the shoulders of the raceway. Five years later, in August of 1938, the "derby" came to Sidney.

Each racer had to be constructed in compliance with rules defined by the Technical Committee of the National Soap Box Derby organization. The details resembled an introductory course in auto mechanics: the front axle tree rotates on a center bolt; rotation is controlled by a wooden tiller; the degree of the turn will be governed by the length of the tongue; and the tongue length must be adjusted to the design of the car. The total cost of construction material could not exceed $10, not counting any items obtained from a "scrapheap or junk pile."

Public excitement mounted as the competition, touted as the "greatest amateur-racing event in the world," drew nearer and nearer. Once the North Main Avenue hill had been chosen as the race site, the State Highway Department graced it with a new coat of tar and gravel and rolled out any rough spots. Organizers conducted test runs, constructed a starting ramp and erected signs directing northbound Dixie Highway traffic onto Ohio Avenue. The weather was a worry, but Mother Nature cooperated.

The big day finally arrived. Twenty-eight cars were registered in two classes. The A group would compete the first day, and the B group the second. Twenty-five hundred people lined the roadway, and judges Mayor John Sexauer, Harry Forsyth and C. D. Beck checked and double-checked their stopwatches. When all the dust and flying gravel had settled and the yelling and cheering had finally ceased, Harry Boblit Jr., of 834 Fielding Road was presented with the first place silver trophy and the opportunity to represent Sidney at Derby Downs in Akron on August 14. His winning time for the 1,100-foot-long run was 42.2 seconds, roughly equivalent to an average speed of 15 miles per hour.

At Akron, Harry Boblit was edged out by less than a car length by Doyle Bracewell of Des Moines in the 14th heat of the national finals. Described by the *Sidney Daily News* reporter as "thrown by the fortunes of the draw into one of the fastest heats of the opening round," Boblit achieved an official time of 29.47 seconds, with the Bracewell vehicle crossing the line at 29.42 seconds, a trivial 0.05 seconds faster. A crowd of more than 100,000 people then watched Robert Berger of Omaha take home the 4-year college scholarship in a photo-finish race. One week later, the Sidney Kiwanis Club voted to sponsor a 1939 race and "motion pictures of the Sidney event taken by Ray Anderson" were shown during the regular luncheon meeting.

All in all, 1938 was quite a year. The fog of war was gathering on the global scene and national sensitivities were being stirred by a variety of far-flung and disturbing news items. Locally, however, the events that would darkly define the next seven years had yet to cast a shadow over Shelby County. There, the wings of an aircraft carrying airmail and the wheels of a racing soapbox formed the focused attention of a community and a people still at peace in a rural environment.

DISCREPANCIES OF HUMANITY

The criminal element has been a part of the human agenda since written communication began to record human activity. The pages of history present a litany of nefarious actors from fanatic medieval knights to today's "white-collar" criminals who steal personal identity files.

Criminal investigation procedures began to undergo drastic changes in the years following the Civil War, when science became an integral part of everyday police work. During the 1870s, Alphonse Bertillon, a French police officer, perfected the use of chemical compounds used to preserve footprints and improved the dynamometer, a device helpful in quantifying the degree of force used in the act of breaking and entering. Dr. Henry Faulds, a Scottish surgeon, published a paper in 1880 that discussed the usefulness of fingerprints for identification, and six years later Thomas Byrnes, head of the New York City police department, published the first "Rogues Gallery," a photographic record of known criminals. In 1889, Alexandre Lacassagne, a French physician, was recognized for pioneering work in bloodstain pattern analysis and his attempts to link spent bullets to specific gun barrels. By 1890 the science of forensics was being widely employed in the continuing fight against crime.

Since its creation in 1819, Shelby County has not escaped the waves of crime that on a small scale operate everywhere on a daily basis and on a larger scale periodically sweep across the horizon of every county in America. The examples presented here range from the horrific to the incomprehensible, including one associated with the greatest of all losses -- one's reputation. The final episode focuses on a genre of crime that is generally even today unrecognized: mankind's indifference to his ignoring the established rules of Mother Nature.

TOO BIG TO FAIL

The epic financial crisis that began in 2008 was a wake-up call to America, at both the hometown and the corporate level. Considered the worst economic calamity since The Great Depression of the 1930s, it resulted in the collapse of more than 450 financial institutions, the widespread bailout of banks by national governments, and severe declines in stock market values around the world. Business failures abounded, consumer wealth loss measured in the billions of dollars, and the general decline in economic activity lead to a global recession. Individuals born during the boom years following World War II faced for the first time a lasting realization that Wall Street was home to not only the proverbial charging "bull," but also the slumbering "bear."

The immediate cause of the crisis in the United States was the collapse of the housing "bubble," which reached a peak around 2006. Default rates on so-called subprime and adjustable-rate mortgages increased as commercial banks approved ever-larger loans to potential homeowners, many of whom could not have qualified under former, more restrictive terms. Mortgage rates declined, housing prices increased and the "bubble" expanded until it imploded.

Some of the most prestigious organizations associated with the American banking industry sadly reached a turning point in their once illustrious history. Marquee names such as Bear Stearns, Merrill Lynch, Lehman

Brothers and Washington Mutual became synonymous with whispered accounts of greed, incompetence and weakened corporate ethical codes. Many surviving institutions, so large and so interconnected that their failure would supposedly be disastrous to the economy, were packaged together by government and industrial economists under the colloquial term "too big to fail." Charge was met with counter-charge as Americans began to publically express the feeling the "American dream" had been replaced by an enduring nightmare.

Within a matter of months the effects of "The Great Recession," reached into the very crossroads of Shelby County, as well as those of the other 3,143 counties and county-equivalent jurisdictions that define the United States of America. Prudence and indecision replaced lifestyles formally conducted with lackadaisical attitudes. Many a citizen surely feared crises of undefined and unprecedented dimensions were to be faced, but those feelings, of course, were only a reflection of their youth. Old timers spoke guardedly of the difficult times of the 1930s and, reaching even further back in time, recalled perhaps the worst economic failure ever to have affected Shelby County -- the 1904 collapse of the German American Bank.

In 1864, the First National Bank became the initial financial institution of record in Shelby County. Eleven years later, two of its front-office employees, Charles Weaver and John Wagner, turned in their resignations and developed plans for the establishment of a new enterprise. Organized as a partnership under the leadership of president Benjamin W. Maxwell, the German American Bank opened its doors on May  1, 1875. Charles C. Weaver served as Vice President and John H. Wagner assumed the role of Cashier. Popular amongst the many German immigrants that populated the city and farmlands of west-central Ohio, the bank was early on burnished with pride and fiscal stamina. Three decades later, however, the once stalwart fixture was an empty building facing the north side of the courthouse, bereft of resource, community support and a future.

William Binkley, editor of *The Sidney Journal*, wrote nostalgically of its early reputation in an August 1904 article:

The failure of the German American Bank is a calamity not only to those directly and personally interested, but also to the whole community. For thirty years it was prominently identified with all that was best for the city and the county. From the beginning its policy was liberal and the management characterized by courteous treatment of its patrons. The business it did in the city and county was very extensive. It is no reflection upon other institutions to say that for many years, perhaps up to the day it closed, its financial transactions were the largest of any in the city. The kindly, undemonstrative manners of the officials and the unquestioned confidences in their integrity accounted for the popularity of the bank...let us not forget that our fallen friends contributed largely to past prosperity and present resources.

Seven months later, with court proceedings still under way and many once-guarded habits of daily bank operation now a matter of public record, Binkley firmly readdressed the public feelings with words that speak succinctly of the tenure of the times:

The efforts to close up the affairs of the German American Bank are dragging their slow lengths along indeed, very much like the proverbial wounded snake. Whatever may be said about the peculiarly loose and incompetent methods of the former popular managers, there are some singularly ludicrous and incongruous manifestations among the patrons of the bank since failure. Fully ninety percent of them knew for years of certain daily habits indulged in by those in control and their subordinates. The extravagances in personal expenditures, rich furnishings, jewels, fine horses and carriages, summer homes, etc., were familiar to everyone. As long, however, as a liberal rate of interest was promised and the generous accommodations granted which characterized the management nobody uttered a word of criticism nor complaint. Things are different now. The same classes are hounding their former benefactors. They are crying for blood. They are hanging around the judicial examinations like hungry wolves, or foul buzzards about a decaying carcass. They are holding up to humiliation and shame their former friends and advertising the extravagances so freely ignored as the cause of the collapse. In the meantime sensible people are saying these patrons sinned away their day of grace. They had knowledge and acted in the face of it, and now common decency would suggest they keep quiet and swallow their losses without murmur. By every rule of law and justice they are stopped by their silence when they should have protested. Queer world, this.

At precisely 2:00 PM, Wednesday, August 24, 1904, the information was made public in a succinct statement that left little doubt in the reader's mind: "The German American Bank failed to open its doors this morning . . .the bank is unable to meet its obligations as they are coming due."

H. T. Mathers
Photograph compliments of Sidney Historical Society

In the early hours of the morning Frank D. Reed, Cashier of the bank, had filed suit against John H. Wagner, President, and the other 17 stockholders of the privately held and now insolvent institution, asking for the appointment of a receiver. The request was heard by Judge H. T. Mathers, and by mid-afternoon W. H. C. Goode had been appointed receiver with his bond guaranteed at $500,000. Hours later, four of the principal stockholders, John Wagner, Frank Reed, Peter Wagner and Mrs. Mary A. Reed made assignments for the benefit of their creditors. Thus began a nine-month-long trial that the *Sidney Daily News* would later describe as "one of the most remarkable cases in the history of Ohio banking."

The 25-paragraph-long news statement was couched mostly in legal jargon but ended with information that quickly became the buzz of the town: the two principals, Mr. Wagner and Mr. Reed were, respectively, "confined to his bed all day to-day," and "confined to his home all day."

In its regular Friday issue, *The Sidney Journal* cut through all the legalese with a sharpened editorial pencil and published its version of the public reaction:

As the day advanced and people were going to their places of business or work the startling fact spread with lightning rapidity, and was soon the absorbing topic of talk in the street and at the fireside. Most naturally, the failure made a profound sensation. So far as the general public was concerned, the crash was a complete surprise. The bank had unlimited confidence and an unusually large number of good depositors. The officers were wealthy and influential members of the community, and above the faintest suspicion as to probity. Their home lives were exemplary, and their friends legion. Though the blow came with crushing effect on the struggling businessman, the provident and hard working farmer, the aged and infirm, the widow and orphan, good sense was in evidence everywhere. People did not become excited. Feelings gave vent to tears, but no threats. Reason, moderation and patience were counseled alike by the fortunate and unfortunate.

By mid-September the details had become indeed sobering: in light of long-held declarations of a capital stock of $73,500 and a surplus of $109,000, the books now appeared to record cash assets of $125,000 and liabilities estimated to be about $700,000 -- and rising. In this day before the formation of the Federal Deposit Insurance Corporation, the enactment of Social Security, payment of unemployment benefits and other means of buoying up the economy, the situation was indeed "not a very favorable one to contemplate."

Those who had not been depositors could sit back with a sigh of relief, but those who held German American savings books and certificates of deposit could only wonder if the stockholders could satisfy their demands. Rumors began to circulate that the bank might be able to pay out, perhaps at best, 25 cents on the dollar.

When definitive information did become available it seemed to defy belief. Surely there was some mistake, but the facts were undisputable: "there had not been a directors' meeting for several years...the bank was run in a loose, haphazard sort of way...money was loaned without taking the necessary security that banks or even men of ordinary prudence would for one moment think of taking.

. .some of the money was loaned in a manner that approximated criminal neglect."

A large crowd of creditors filled the assembly room of the courthouse on Saturday afternoon and listened to a proposition of a 25 percent payout as suggested by David Oldham, attorney for the bank, but the offer was rejected without a single dissenting vote. Still, questions abounded: "Where did the money go?" and "Who are the parties that are guilty of the breach of trust, or to put it plainly, who stole the money?" On Monday morning, as soon as the bankruptcy petition had been filed in the Federal Court in Cincinnati, Judge A. C. Thompson Friday hinted at an answer by ordering the bank assets and title to Frank Reed's rural cottage be legally secured.

John Wagner took the stand in early February 1905 and under sworn testimony revealed for the first time information that sent a financial seismic wave throughout Sidney and Shelby County. He testified that in spite of the fact "he knew stealing was going on for ten or twelve years. . .they kept no check on the cash at the bank. . .had not been counting it. . .at one time a check for 72 cents was paid out for $72. . .efforts were made to locate the thief or thieves. . .he became discouraged." Having said all that, he then assured the court "he had followed up on employees who were spending more money than their salary should allow but could not find out who did the stealing."

The following day Frank Reed took the stand and commenced to tell a tale that defined a banking environment of chicanery and nonchalance conveniently enveloped within a sense of unprecedented serenity. "When he began as cashier the cash was all right," he reported but "he quit counting years ago when it got so mixed he could not tell head or tail about it." Pausing for breath, he informed the massed audience that "he made up the dividends . . .according to instructions by giving 4 percent semi-annually on each share of stock. . .the dividend had no relation to the earnings of the bank." He had, however, "nothing to do with swelling the surplus. . .Wagner did that." In conclusion, he revealed he "did not know much about the bank. . .but did "give his wife cash when she wanted it and got the cash out of the bank on his check."

On the evening of February 24 Reed was placed under arrest in Toledo, and the next morning Wagner was arrested in Sidney by Chief of Police William O'Leary. Both men were charged with embezzlement. One month later they stood before Judge Mathers in Common Pleas Court as the indictments were read into the record: nine for embezzlement and three for obtaining money under false pretenses against Wagner and eight against Reed, all for embezzlement.

Eventually, motions were filed to quash certain of the indictments on the basis they "do not state with sufficient definiteness and certainty the facts to support the conclusions." The men were fighting in concert to retain some shreds of their former reputations, but as reported by the press their demeanor in court showed they were reacting to the continuing procedures on an individual basis: Reed "did not appear to feel the embarrassment of the situation," while "Wagner had gotten up from a sick bed to come to Court and showed both mental and physical sufferings."

In May the final act in the bankruptcy proceedings took place. All of the properties owned by the defunct establishment, as well as those of the responsible stockholders, were sold. The success of the three-day event, as evidenced by receipts that totaled almost $120,000, gave reason for the *Sidney Daily News* to express its view of the future to a reading public that was still reeling in lingering degrees of disbelief:

> When the German American Bank failed nine months ago our people felt we had received a blow that would embarrass us for years, and it is true many of our people in the country as well as the city were hit hard. In many parts of the state we were spoken of patronizingly as suffering irreparable losses. But it was not so. Where there is a will there is a way. Our people have the will and they choose the way by going to work with redoubled energy that had produced satisfactory results. Our obligations are promptly met and business was never better with us than now.

ALBERT DICKAS

The bankruptcy of the German American bank is now but a distant, near forgotten, memory. The episode will long remain, however, in the annals of Shelby County history testimony that in spite of the conceived significance of any institution or organization, none becomes too big to fail.

ENVIRONMENTS OF MAYHEM

In the *History of Shelby County*, published in 1883 by R. Sutton and Company, the reader is given a brief insight into the prevailing social and intellectual conditions that defined that period of time midway between the end of the horrors of a Civil War and the rising effervescence associated with the dawning of a new century:

> Perhaps it was a rude culture which obtained for the time; perhaps it was a rude community, perhaps the temples of education, justice, and religion were rude, but above and below, within and without that rudeness, the spirit at its very best was manifested.

An example of "the spirit at its very best" is given in the final portion of this volume in an 1892 reminiscence published by William Binkley, editor of *The Sidney Journal*. It is a litany of individuals who through their lives had given leadership and progressive continuity to Sidney and Shelby County during the preceding quarter century. The listing is the bright side of regional human history that might very well be described as one of "par excellence."

But what of the other side, the reverse, the shadowy "rude" side of human nature? Just as a coin must have two faces, so does any rendition of local history and the population of persons who make that history.

During the time between 1870 and 1895, a quarter of a century that very nearly coincides with the time period covered in the 1892 article printed by William Binkley, six vicious acts of mayhem took place within the overall confines of Shelby County. In their settings and chains of circumstances, each typifies a time when daily life was controlled by local rather than national events, travel was limited to rail, canal or carriage and information was distributed by word of mouth and a weekly press.

DEATH IN A DITCH

With a blast of its whistle and the release of a massive cloud of steam, the long freight train moved slowly across the Great Miami River bridge on the morning of Monday, February 26, 1872, gained speed as it passed the area of Tawawa Lake and continued eastbound over the tracks of the Cleveland, Cincinnati, Chicago and St. Louis Railway. Two miles later, approaching the rail crossing of the north-south pike connecting Pasco with Port Jefferson in Perry Township, the high-powered locomotive light illuminated a sight most certainly not normal to any rail right-of-way. In the ditch along the south side of the track lay the body of a man, encased in a temporary tomb of ice. Authorities were called, and identification was quickly established.

Levi Carbaugh was an industrious and frugal young man who made a living working on the nearby farm of John and Norman Key. His death had been caused by a bullet to his head and the thrust of a knife across his throat. Summoned to the scene, John Key identified the corpse and informed the authorities Levi had held a note for wages due, in the amount of $116, against his son Norman Key, but had recently sold it to another of the Key farmhands, one Zacharias Medaris. Upon questioning, Medaris confirmed the note transfer, saying it had been all but paid except for $10.

Investigations revealed that both farmhands had left their place of residence at about the same time. Carbaugh was bound for Norman's house with pockets flush with a fair amount of money while Medaris volunteered his intent was to visit his ailing mother.

Upon the discovery of blood on Medaris's trousers and an unexpected

$50 among his personal belongings, he was arrested and confined to the Shelby County jail.

During the trial, the State contended the victim had proceeded due east to the Pasco railroad crossing after leaving the Key homestead without knowing he was being pursued by Medaris. When he caught up, Medaris murdered Carbaugh, robbed him and threw the body in the ditch, partly concealing it with foliage.

The prosecution's case was backed up by testimony from two inmates who had overheard Medaris confessing the crime to his brother and by an Ohio State chemist who confirmed the confiscated trousers were indeed stained by human blood. Witnesses called by the defense proved to be of questionable reputation, and their testimony was shown to be without foundation. The jury recessed and within a half hour returned with a verdict of "not guilty." The surprise decision was the result of one member of the jury voting for acquittal and then allegedly bullying the others into agreement. Medaris was a free man, but it was not long before he was again arrested, charged with the crime of forgery. This time found guilty, he was sent to the Ohio State penitentiary for two years.

Death by a Bludgeon

William Schnapp is the victim in this particular case. Little is known of him, beyond the fact he resided in Newberry Township, Miami County and spent at least some of his time collecting rents for his father, the owner of various farm properties throughout the region.

On the day of the crime, Tuesday, November 9, 1875, Schnapp, accompanied by his friend Frank P. Turney, was in Loramie Township, Shelby County, hoping to collect rent due from John Riddle. Riddle, known to have a hot temper, was in the act of closing the barn doors, assisted by his half-brother B. F. Stover. Carrying the proverbial big chip on his shoulder at that very moment, Riddle snarled to Turney that while he had no ill feelings against him, he should stay outside because he wanted to conduct the rent payment with Schnapp in private, calling Schnapp at the same time "that dirty dog."

Schnapp angerly reacted, "Don't you call me that." Riddle lunged while simultaneously calling for Stover to hand him a club lying in the corner of the barnyard. In spite of Turney's best efforts to intercede, Stover passed the wooden bludgeon to Riddle who viscously beat Schnapp on his head and then turned his attack on Turney. With Turney on the run, Riddle went into the house, returned with a hammer and noisily cleared the yard with threats of more violence.

Turney managed to get Schnapp back to his home alive. A careful examination of the wounds revealed them to be too serious for amateur care, so a physician was called, but two hours after his arrival Schnapp died. At the trial, conducted in May 1876 before Judge James MacKenzie, Riddle was convicted of murder in the second degree and sentenced to the Ohio State Penitentiary for life. For his part in the episode, B. F. Stover was tried and also sentenced. Several years later, Riddle exercised his violent temper again by assaulting and killing a fellow prisoner.

The year 1880 was long remembered as the year of crime in Shelby County, because three murders were recorded between March and September, "each successive one being worse than its predecessor." Two of the victims were female and, as in the case of eight years earlier, the scene of the third took place in conjunction with a freight train of the C. C. C. and St. Louis line.

DEATH BY A REVOLVER

Apparently it was a custom of the time. A freight train, by definition, does not carry passengers, but for the standard fare a few travelers were permitted transit in the caboose. It was Tuesday, April 6, 1880, and the Big Four freight was headed west out of Sidney. When the conductor asked for payment of $1.05 for transport to Union City on the Ohio/Indiana border, the "strong, sturdy looking man . . . of very swarthy complexion" replied he had neither money nor intention to pay if he had. Put off the train, he immediately climbed back on and just as quickly was again discharged. Once more gaining entry, he pulled his revolver and fired. The bullet, intended for the conductor, instead hit Joseph M. Lehman, en route from Quincy to Houston. Struck above the left eye, Lehman fell to the caboose floor and died within a matter of seconds. The murderer escaped into the nearby woods.

In due time a suspicious character was discovered, and upon questioning gave the name of Conrad Reutebach, of St. Henry. Identified by several witnesses to the crime, and unable to adequately describe his whereabouts when Lehman was shot, Reutebach was arrested. At his September trial, it was learned the moniker Reutebach was an alias and his real name was John Walker. Without ever admitting any knowledge of the crime and all the while maintaining his innocence, Walker was found guilty and sentenced to be hanged. After his office had received numerous petitions from individuals who claimed the testimony was far from conclusive, Governor Charles William Foster subsequently changed, at the eleventh hour, his sentence to life imprisonment. Pardoned five years later, Walker reportedly gave considered thought to the real value of $1.05 and "since then has borne an excellent reputation."

DEATH BY HALLUCINATION

Since it was a nice morning, that Friday, June 18, 1880, Mrs. Ann Line paid a visit to her Perry Township neighbor Mrs. Ellen Inskeep. As they shared gossip, a young man by the name of David Shanks approached on foot from the direction of Port Jefferson. He sternly inquired what Mrs. Line was doing. When she answered, "paying a visit," he considered the reply insolent and quizzically intoned with decided authority, "I am God Almighty, Father, Son and Spirit, and I say depart, be unkind, my curse be upon you."

When Shanks then pulled the chair out from under Mrs. Line, Mrs. Inskeep ran to the rescue and the entire scene became one of pandemonium. Chasing the scrambling ladies, Shanks caught up with Mrs. Line, threw her to the ground, "deliberately beat in her head with a piece of fence rail" and made his escape off to the west. Following a massive search, he was eventually found immersed in the cold waters of the Great Miami River, stark naked. At his trial he answered to the name of Christ and testified he was drunk at the time and guilty only of killing Jefferson Davis, the former president of the Confederate States of America, in supposed response to Davis' being guilty of killing Mrs.

Line. Found to have been subject for years to "hallucinations and mania" and with a history of threats to various individuals, he was sentenced to life imprisonment. His pardon was granted in 1892.

DEATH ALONG THE CANAL

The body, female, decidedly pregnant and with a shattered skull, was discovered on the morning of Wednesday, August 25, 1880, along the bank of the Feeder Canal between Sidney and Port Jefferson and identified as Mrs. William Curtis. There was a surplus of evidence that she had put up a fierce struggle before being killed with a fence post, a weapon termed "the customary one in Shelby County" by *The Sidney Journal*. In no time at all, the captain of the canal boat "Night Hawk" publically announced he had found blood stains on certain items belonging to one of his employees, the husband of the victim. Arrested, William Curtis feigned confusion when he saw the corpse, claiming it might be that of his wife's sister.

The facts of the case presented during the trial revealed Mrs. Curtis had been visiting at the home of a friend near Dayton. A few days prior to the crime Mr. Curtis hired a horse and buggy from the livery in Port Jefferson and said he was going to bring his wife home.

Several individuals were witness to the fact the couple purchased a quantity of oats when they arrived in Troy. Soon thereafter they began to argue. They were later seen driving through Sidney, but there the trail was lost. Investigation of the crime found a scattering of oats on the floor of the rented buggy and also around the canal bank where the body had been discovered -- prima-facie evidence of murder most foul. Convicted of murder in the second degree, Curtis was sentenced to life in the state penitentiary.

PASSAGES

DEATH BY A PALING

On that particular night of Wednesday, October 11, 1893, nothing seemed out of the ordinary as the sun set over the small community of Pemberton, but all that changed at 10:15. Mrs. Archibald Davidson was suddenly awakened from her slumber by the sound of a series of heavy blows accompanied by a shrill voice demanding the Almighty to immediately bring retribution down upon some poor soul. When she ran to the window, she could just make out the shadowy form of a man tiptoeing across the yard and heard a litany of "low, gurgling groans" coming from a short distance up the road.

In no time at all, Mrs. Davidson was joined by her husband and Homer Spence, who also slept in the house. They in turn aroused some neighbors, Joshua Cox, his two sons and Jacob Cost, and together the unauthorized posse began an investigation. Eighty feet up the road they came across the body of Isaac N. Ray, known to all as a 47-year-old bachelor who worked at Moore's livery stable and lived a simple and peaceful life with his 84-year-old mother. Nearby lay the murder weapon, a three-foot-long piece of paling, one of a row of upright, pointed sticks that form a fence. One end was charred and whittled down so as to "afford a grip for the fingers." The skull was crushed by a fracture that ran from the forehead and across the top to the back.

In the brilliant light of morning a full-fledged inquiry began in a case known more for its questions than its answers. No motive was ever determined and no suspect was ever identified. Ray was a quiet, inoffensive man with no known enemies. Rewards totaling $700 were offered for the arrest of the murderer, but the money remained unclaimed in a crime *The Sidney Journal* finally labeled "The Pemberton Mystery."

Today, crime reports in the press, on the web and on television are so prevalent there is a general feeling that 21st century life in America is overwhelmed with acts of wanton destruction and violent disorder. Yet, as the details of the above half-dozen crimes indicate, life during the latter decades of the 19th century in Shelby County, when its population was half of what it is today, was most certainly not one of harmonious relations and pastoral quietude. It might thus be said that the wordings in the *History of Shelby County* was, conceivably, not far off the mark when the local environment of 1883 was described as . . ."perhaps it was a rude culture which obtained for the time."

PROSECUTION AND ACQUITTAL

Along with the prospect of religious freedom and the desire to escape from the tyrannical policies of Old World European governments, visions of land ownership on a grand scale or fortunes made in pursuit of a craft or trade fueled emigration to the New World. Clearly, such grandiose concepts of wealth and prosperity required someone to work the land, as the economic foundation of the budding colonies was the potential associated with its hundreds of thousands of square miles of virgin soil. National growth and progress was therefore enhanced by the presence and manipulation of slaves, indentured peoples without hope or rights. To this end, pirated African nationalities were first enslaved in America during the early days of colonization in the 17th century.

Slavery in the South, historically defined as lands lying south of the Ohio River and the Mason Dixon Line, became critical in the half-dozen years leading up to 1800. The climate was especially adaptable to the growing of cotton, but once the harvest was gathered seeds had to be manually removed from the cotton fibers, a labor-intensive and expensive process. With the invention of the cotton gin, however, this crop became unusually profitable, and acreage planted in cotton was increased multifold, producing a need for ever more pickers. The South thus became a rural and plantation-based society, heavily indebted to the concept of human servitude.

In the North, slavery was also present from the earliest days of colonization, but on a smaller scale since the society was, compared to its southern neighbors, more urban and industrially oriented. Estates of 50 slaves were unusual, and the average slave-owning Atlantic seaboard household counted less than a handful of slaves.

Following the years of the Revolutionary War this situation changed, as anti-slavery legislation was passed in all of the Yankee states. Soon, virtually all African-related minorities living in the North were considered part and parcel of so-called "free-black populations," whose count numbered almost 50,000 by 1810.

Slavery was legally abolished in the Northwest Territory in 1802. This did not necessarily mean, however, freedom for its black population or an improvement in the process of immigration out of Kentucky, the slave state lying immediately on the other side of the Ohio River. In both 1804 and 1807 legislation was approved in Ohio that required entering blacks to post bond of $500 guaranteeing a strictly defined behavior and possession of court-approved documentation proving they were free.

When a community of 383 slaves was set free following the death of Virginian John Randolph of Roanoke, the hospitality of Ohio was severely tested. Moving by wagon, riverboat and canal barge across a distance of nearly 500 miles in the summer of 1846, these freemen set their sights on Carthagena, a Mercer County, Ohio community founded 11 years before for the express purpose of becoming a refuge for freed slaves from the South. Unfortunately, such expectations were not to be. As *The Sidney Journal* later reported; when "a boat carrying as passengers ... about 100 Randolph slaves ... passed up to the vicinity of Berlin (Ft. Loramie) but were not allowed to land ... a mob received them with sticks and stones." Their search for equality halted by prejudice and fear, the travelers began to scatter to nearby communities.

Some of the Randolph slaves ended up in Rumley, a predominantly African-American community platted in 1837 along the stage route connecting Piqua and Lima. In its hey day the population numbered some 500 persons, but today the only evidence of this once viable Shelby County community is a Baptist church and Collins Cemetery clustered two miles northeast of McCartyville. One particular individual, however, Alfred Artis, a member of the small group of Randolph slaves who populated Rumley, was destined to make Shelby County history.

TRIAL AND CONVICTION

Alfred Artis was not one of the most beloved of individuals. Feared by just about all of his Van Buren Township neighbors, he lived for the most part isolated from society on his farm of 130 acres, near Rumley, in uneven harmony with his wife and several children. His relationship with his oldest daughter, 15-year-old Emma, was especially difficult. He often railed that a stubborn disposition was behind her refusal to chop wood, pick up brush and work in the fields. She died on February 17, 1854, after being subjected to numerous acts of torture over a three-month period -- chained in an unheated room and forced to work outside until her hands and feet were frostbitten. Court records state Emma's body was found in her father's house. Alfred was charged with murder in the first degree, the first such capital case recorded in Shelby County history.

Isaac Harshbarger, the county coroner, held the inquest into the case and the grand jury met on April 21. On July 6, the trial began in the old 44-foot-square, 2-story, brick courthouse constructed in the center of the square a little over two decades earlier. Following two days of testimony by seven witnesses, plus Rhoda Artis' testimony that she had been raped a year earlier by her father, the 12-man jury reported it was unable to reach a decisive verdict. The community reacted with shock and anger, and a new trial was ordered. Four months later, a newly impaneled 12-man jury reached agreement following a day of testimony and deliberation -- guilty as charged. Artis was sentenced to death by hanging and confined to jail until the day of execution. Over a thousand persons visited his cell prior to his execution, most of whom wished merely to cast eyes on him out of a sense of curiosity.

To this day, the details of the precise surroundings of the hanging remain shrouded in a veil of confusion. In his book *Voices From the Past*, Rich Wallace says Artis died on a gallows constructed "on the southwest corner of the courtsquare" as "Sheriff Dryden then did his duty before a large crowd" and was "paid the substantial sum of $300 for his work." The *Shelby County Democrat*, however, in a review of the Artis murder case published on May 3, 1907, reported:

> The hanging took place in the old brick jail that stood in the southwest corner of the public square. The scaffold was erected in the hallway in the old jail and the hanging was witnessed by only a few persons. However, on the outside there was an enormous crowd . . . the largest crowd that was ever in Sidney.

Whatever the details, there is unanimity regarding the environment of the hanging. In his mid-thirties, Alfred was incredibly strong, even though he weighed in at a relatively light 130 pounds. As the hour of execution arrived, he refused to cooperate, and it took the combined effort of four men -- Sheriff J. C. Dryden, Isaac Harshbarger (by now the deputy sheriff), William Snaveley and Robinson Joslin -- and the better part of 30 minutes to wrestle him out of his cell and along the hallway to the gallows. Struggling every foot of the way, he was finally manhandled up the steps to the platform where the rope noose was placed around his neck.

At approximately 10:40 on the morning of February 23, 1855, Alfred Artis was pronounced dead. The body was cut down and confined in a common casket that "was placed out in the center of the street in front of the jail and the people given an opportunity to view the body." Later, it was removed to his Van Buren farm, laid in a casket and buried in a wooded area.

Many aspects of this case are bothersome when compared to present-day trial procedures. It is not known whether the accused was ever allowed legal counsel during the trial, his fate was placed in the hearts and minds of an all-white jury, he was reportedly beaten to insensibility because of his resistance at the hour of execution and the presiding judge overruled a motion to change venue. Whatever the facts, and many have been lost within the mists of time, the tale of the Alfred Artis episode will forever remain a sad and shadowy chapter in the history of Sidney and Shelby County.

Trial and Acquittal

Prior to the advent of the Civil War, Ohio played a significant role in the establishment and operation of the Underground Railroad, a diverse system of safe houses and shadowy byways that connected the states of the slave-holding South with communities of freedom in Canada. It has been estimated that some 3,000 miles of Underground Railroad trails ran through Ohio. Mileage contained in Shelby County progressed northeast from Piqua and then diverged in the vicinity of Lockington into three courses: one following the route of the Miami and Erie Canal to Toledo, another paralleling present day I-75 north to Wapakoneta and the third meandering through wooded back country leading to Kenton.

In spite of its intimate association with the Underground Railroad, the designation of Ohio as a "free state" did not necessarily mean it was friendly to those migrating persons of color. Pro-slavery organizations were active in many areas, and many an individual made a living as a bounty hunter. Under the early laws of the state, African American males could not enlist in the military, hope to send their children to public-supported schools, serve on juries or testify against white citizens in a court of law. Supposedly the outcome of the Civil War brought an end to these racially-motivated restrictions, but such was not the case, as evidenced by an advertisement dated September 15, 1865, which appeared in Sidney newspapers:

WARNING to Negroes in Shelby County

> ... in consequence of the late influx of Negroes to some parts of this county ... and in consequence of their bad conduct, insolence, and competition with white labor ... it was resolved to give you warning that you must arrange your business and depart within sixty days from this date ... or measures already adopted will be taken to make this location unhealthy for you. Our means are adequate.

With the continuing passage of time, the rights of the Black population underwent trials of process and regression. The 1868 adoption of the 14th Amendment to the Constitution of the United States was a significant step forward by bestowing citizenship upon all former slaves and granting them equal protection of the laws. Counteracting this progressive legislation, however, was the spawning of the Ku Klux Klan, the end of Reconstruction in the 1870s and the continuation of an environment of poverty and racism that shadowed the daily life of most persons of color. Such were the circumstances when a second murder trial was held in Shelby County, again involving a member of that small band of Randolph slaves who had migrated north from Virginia in 1846.

Shadrack White was not his real name. Perhaps even he did not know his real name, since he was born a slave. On a compiled list of Blacks freed by the will of "John Randolph of Roanoke" he is listed as #514 -- Shadrack -- 5 feet, 3.5 inches tall and 50 years old. Settling into a new life in Sidney, he took the surname White, but throughout the remainder of his life he was known simply and fondly as "Buddie Shang." Lacyburg, a squalid Fourth Ward shantytown community of a dozen or more hovels located south of Water Street, along the trace of the Miami and Erie feeder canal, was his home.

On October 31, 1889, Shang, described by *The Sidney Journal*, as "a peaceable vagrant, and not sound in mind, who has not done a day's work for years, and who lived by hunting and fishing, got his clothes for nothing and his whisky by gathering mint for saloons," was walking along the towpath pleasantly singing and carrying his double-barreled shotgun. Suddenly calm turned to crisis, a brick or two was thrown, charge and countercharge issued and shots were fired. When the smoke cleared, Lewis "Soapstick" Nichols, a white, Civil War veteran described in the same newspaper account as "an idle, worthless, vicious, drinking man without a redeeming quality," lay dying on the ground with multiple wounds in his right shoulder. Shang reportedly made no attempt at all to escape.

The trial began on Monday, January 27, 1890, almost three months after the day of the killing. The prosecution claimed Shang acted out of malice and in a state of mind of provocation, whereas the defense called a number of witnesses, all of whom testified to the good character of the defendant. As soon as the all-white, male jury departed for their deliberation, the audience, reportedly the largest ever to have assembled in a Sidney courtroom, "tendered the defendant an informal reception." Some 25 minutes later, the verdict was delivered by the foreman -- not guilty -- and the room erupted in yells of approval. Shang was for the second time in his life declared a freeman, initially by John Randolph of Roanoke and now by the citizens of Sidney and Shelby County. In his report of the trial, *The Sidney Journal* editor concluded:

> . . . we would suggest to all those persons who heretofore have abused him by practical jokes and by getting him intoxicated should refrain from doing so in the future. If this is done there will be no more unfortunate occurrences such as Shang has just emerged from. His disposition is to remain perfectly quiet and peaceable, and he must be let alone if he should be on the streets again.

In late March 1912, the *Sidney Daily News* reported that Shang, suffering for some time from the effects of a broken leg, had passed away at the County Infirmary. Some reports indicated he was 97 years old.

In both of these celebrated cases of murder the accused was, from the standpoint of all documented evidence, guilty. Two trials were required to find Alfred Artis culpable, perhaps because the jury recognized improprieties associated with the first. In the case of the State of Ohio vs. Shadrach White, the jury was obviously guided by the heart, rather than the mind.

Over the gap of nearly four decades, two black men were judged in a legally constituted trial by an all-white jury. Looking back on the outcome of these 19th century events, it would seem that the citizens of Shelby County did not at the time harbor an invasive attitude of racial profiling or discrimination.

MURDER MOST MERCENARY

Located in the upper left hand corner of an inside page, the January 31, 1915, notice in the *Sidney Daily News* wasn't very long: 170 words compressed into three paragraphs. An inmate serving a life sentence for murder at the state penitentiary in Columbus had nonchalantly walked away from an honor squad at the prison farm and was, as the saying goes in the law enforcement business, "at large."

To the average reader this was no big deal, until the name of Frank Walker was mentioned. Yes, yes, remember some eight years ago, the very same Frank Walker was found guilty of second-degree murder in a case *The Sidney Journal-Gazette* headlined as "ATROCIOUS," and a "GREAT SHOCK TO THE CITY."

The news of the day was not at all unusual so far as the residents of the city and county were concerned. President Theodore Roosevelt was suggesting future elections be paid for by the national government and not by private contributions; local wheat prices were down, another example of supply and demand; Sidney was to be soon graced by two new bridges over the Miami and Erie canal feeder, a single-span high truss crossing on the Nutt county road and a re-enforced concrete arch on Poplar Street; and the Ringling Brothers circus was scheduled to arrive in Piqua in ten days. On Saturday, April 20, however, the tranquility of the season was shattered by events that were headlined "Fellow Townsman and Esteemed Citizen . . . Shot Down . . . Cold

Blooded, Premeditated Murder." The year was 1907 and life, at least for the time being, would not be the same, for this "was the first murder that has occurred within our limits in (the) last twenty-five years."

The victim, William B. Legg, a 47-year-old Shelby County native, was born near Houston, where he spent his formative years. At age 14 he moved with his family to the state of Illinois. Imbued with a strong sense of wanderlust, he subsequently spent 20 or more years moving from place to place throughout the Midwest: Kansas, Texas, Colorado, back to Illinois and finally, in 1896, to Sidney. He was employed at the North Miami Avenue plant of the American Wheel Company until fire destroyed that facility one year later. Turning loss to advantage, he had married the former Gertrude Cecil of Hardin and opened a meat market on West Michigan Street. President of the board of trustees of the Christian Endeavor Society and a member in good standing in the Modern American Woodmen Association and the United Brethren church, he was survived by three brothers, as many sisters and his wife.

The perpetrators, two in number, were variously described in the extensive newspaper publicity as tramps, hobos, highwaymen and persons of a "desperate character." Both were reported to possess evidence of a wasted, reckless life and infection by a disease described simply as "loathsome."

Howard West, also known as Thomas Anderson, Howard Dorner, Frank (or Ed) Dalton and Frank Earl, the latter the alias-of-choice during the Sidney robbery, was the son of a Pittsburgh-based railroad telegraph operator, a convicted member of a Cincinnati-based hold-up gang and an itinerate purveyor of small trinkets. An inveterate cigarette and cocaine fiend, when he was arrested he had two nitroglycerine cartridges with 6-inch fuses -- used to blow open safes--sewn into his clothes, in addition to a 38-caliber, serial number 1408 Colt regulation police revolver and a knife in his pocket. A strip search in jail revealed a moneybag containing $15.15 tied to one leg beneath his underwear. Twenty-six years old, he stood 6 feet, 2 inches tall, had a slender build, weighed 165 pounds and wore dark clothes and a stiff hat. If this description had not been enough for a ready identification, the fact he was missing half his left arm -- explained as either the result of a car accident or an accident occurring while he was in jail -- marked him as a man not to be overlooked in a crowd.

At the time of his arrest the second half of this nefarious gang-of-two identified himself as Frank Walker, but his real name was Frank Whiting. Born into a distinguished Illinois family, he continually resisted giving any background information until confronted with the fact he had five accomplished siblings, a sister and four brothers, all of whom apparently considered him the black sheep of the family. Referred to as the "short one" throughout the trial, he stood five feet, seven inches tall, weighed in at 135 pounds, sported a mustache and gave his age as 31 years. When captured he was carrying a 32 caliber, loaded Iver and Johnston pistol, $16.57 in "silver money," and an attitude that smacked of belligerency.

Information regarding the crime committed by the two Franks was published in lurid, contradictory and exhausting detail in the *Shelby County Democrat*, *The Sidney Journal-Gazette* and the *Sidney Daily News*. The devil most certainly was in the details and the truth compounded

Shelby County Courthouse, the site of the 1907 Legg murder trial.

by the differing testimonies of a handful of citizens who witnessed the crime and the often-devious answers the prisoners gave during a series of intensive interrogations described as a "severe grilling" conducted within a "sweating" environment. Eventually, however, a semblance of actuality emerged, the result of good police work, as directed by Chief of Police William O'Leary, and investigative reporting on the part of local newspapermen.

Testimony presented during the trial indicated Walker and Earl had known each other for a week or so, and both were regular passengers on Cincinnati, Hamilton and Dayton freight trains that frequented the western Ohio region. On the day of the crime they left Piqua shortly after sundown and traveled north to Sidney where they spent several hours reconnoitering the neighborhood around the Legg butcher shop and observing the arrival and departure of customers.

Around 10 PM, they decided to make their move, having seen the blinds being lowered and Garney Woodruff, the shop clerk, depart. Earl went first, followed by Walker 20 feet behind, both armed. They hoped to encounter Legg in the back of the store, but met him instead at the front door. When they threatened him, Legg -- described as "no stranger to cowardice" -- struck out with his leg. Two shots rang out and with his last words, "My God, I am shot," the victim fell to the floor dead. One bullet pierced the upper part of his heart, grazed his left arm and passed entirely through his body. The other entered his left hip and coursed upward before it lodged. With the exception of a few pennies, the cash-register money, estimated to total $35 to $50, was missing along with a Citizen's National Bank canvas bag used to carry store receipts to the bank.

Within a matter of minutes, at least a dozen witnesses and a terrified Mrs. Legg had begun to gather in an assembly that ultimately increased to hundreds as the news spread throughout the city by word-of-mouth. Chief of Police O'Leary, convinced the criminals had left the city, initiated a regional dragnet, notifying railroad conductors and law enforcement officials that two alleged murderers were on the loose and dangerous.

Gathering all the money they could, Earl and Walker ran north along the alley adjacent to the meat market, but were quickly confronted by William Murphy a clerk in a nearby grocery owned by Oliver Forrar. Shots were exchanged with little effect, except that within the moonlit situation the burglars were able to further their retreat. Running to the east to the railroad right-of-way, a mere block and a half distant, and then north along the tracks, they rested near a water tank where Earl reloaded his gun. Continuing east to the Western Ohio electric interurban trolley line, they decided to follow these tracks and walk 20 miles north to Wapakoneta.

During the ensuing seven hours, they stopped on three occasions to hide from passing trolley cars. The second time, near Anna and halfway to their destination, they counted the stolen money, divided it and discarded the bank bag near a fence post.

At Wapakoneta they boarded a flat car loaded with railroad ties and rode to Lima where they jumped off, walked through a muddy woods into town, registered at a hotel and ordered breakfast. The sun was rising on a beautiful Sunday morning.

Shortly thereafter, Daniel M. Kelley, a detective on the Lima police force, was making his rounds and noticed two men in the downtown area who appeared to fit the description of suspects the Sidney police department had sent. Approaching them, he asked where they lived. The taller of the two became testy, a scuffle broke out, Kelley delivered an effective fisticuff, and in short order Earl and Walker were under arrest and on the way to jail.

The next morning a sizeable group of officials and witnesses-to-the-crime gathered in the Mayor's office in Lima. After "all their clothes were taken from them" the suspects were brought from their cells, first one and then the other, and the "sweating process began." Walker did most of the talking, but delivered conflicting accounts. In time he weakened and implicated his partner as the one who fired the bullets and thus committed the murder.

A confession secured, authorities arranged for the perpetrators to arrive in Sidney that very night on the 9:45 Western Ohio interurban car. Anticipating a large and perhaps unruly crowd at the jail, Chief

O'Leary and his assistants escorted the accused off the car at the Big Four railroad crossing and stealthily walked the prisoners "east . . . to Miami Avenue, then . . . south to the south side of Court Street and quickly up to the jail," where they put the men in separate cells on separate floors.

Selection of a jury was an extremely drawn out affair, made difficult by the supposed absence of citizens who had not already formed an opinion on the merits of the case. Numerous panels of prospective jurors, in total 107 individuals, were called before attorneys from both sides agreed to an even dozen "good and true" men. In early June the trial of the accused, already arraigned under their alias monikers of Frank Earl and Frank Walker, got under way in the common pleas courtroom in Sidney.

The prosecution presented evidence very much the same as that the three local newspapers had published, with one significant exception. A detailed examination of the crime scene bullets, one found at the time of the murder and the other discovered a day later, indicated they were fired from different guns, rather than the one as originally alleged. One bullet weighed 89 grains, the weight of a 32-caliber weapon, and the other tipped the scales at a hefty 145 grains, evidence it came from a 38-caliber revolver. Both men had shot in quick succession, and both would now stand trial.

The trials can only be described as a whirlwind of courtroom activities, the nature of which kept the public continually salivating for more information. Walker agreed to testify for the state against Earl and changed his initial plea of not guilty to murder in the first degree to a plea of guilty of murder in the second degree. With the ponderous amount of lurid press available to the reading public Earl's lawyers requested a change of venue, but the presiding judge, H. T. Mathers, refused. Finally, a motion for a new trial for Earl, supported by an allegation one juror had expressed bias prior to his selection, was denied.

The jurors found Earl guilty of first-degree murder, and he was sentenced to die in the electric chair at the state penitentiary in Columbus. Having "rendered services to the state" Walker was sentenced to life in prison. The Circuit Court of Appeals overruled the defense lawyers' subsequent attempts to save Earl's life. After the Ohio Supreme Court refused to give further consideration to the case, the chain of legal maneuvers ran out of steam when Governor Andrew L. Harris "on the day before the execution . . . refused to intervene."

In the very first report of the murder, as published in the April 26, 1907, issue of *The Journal-Gazette*, it is interesting to note the reporter editorialized:

> Society must be protected, and the fiend that enters the very portals of the house and takes human life without the least provocation must not complain if the mandates of the law, to protect home and society, is carried out in the electric chair.

The citizens of Sidney and Shelby County apparently had no objection to this strongly worded, albeit grammatically marred, paragraph.

The execution took place during the first moments of Thursday, December 19, under the eyes of 30 witnesses. After "querulously complaining against his wretched fate and bitterly inveighing against those who brought him to its realization," Frank Earl uttered his last words, "I ask God to forgive me for all my sins." As his body was being placed in a willow basket, for transfer to a waiting ambulance, a pencil fell from the pocket of the coat he wore. It was quickly picked up, cut into segments and distributed as souvenirs.

Was it poetic justice or just plain luck when the sharpened pencil point segment, complete with a piece of protruding lead, was secured by Garney Woodruff, Mr. Legg's trusted clerk? Woodruff had traveled to Columbus as the personal representative of the *Sidney Daily News*. In his report he made an interesting observation:

> It is a peculiar circumstance that from the time the murder was committed . . . to the time Earl paid the penalty . . . just eight months to the day had elapsed.

Seven years and six weeks later, Frank Walker walked away from an honor squad at the Columbus prison farm and disappeared into the pages of history. He apparently had decided to take matters into his own hands after the Ohio State Board of Pardons had denied his earlier appeal for parole.

EFFECT AND CAUSE

Weather and its many vagaries have long been both a mystery and a challenge to humanity. Farmers have concerns about how the fluctuating relationships between sunshine and rainfall will affect their annual harvest. Commercial pilots check and doublecheck cloud cover and wind patterns that may cross their planned flight paths. Actuaries constantly update the statistics of hurricane and winter storm cycles. Informed families know to check the Weather Channel before planning a family vacation or a day at the beach. In short, the subject of weather is of interest to almost everyone.

With batteries of satellites focused on Earth on a 24/7 basis, the science of meteorology allows present day life to be lived on a more predictable basis than what was possible in former decades. Take, for example, the vague forecast from a 1936 edition of the *Sidney Daily News*: "Lower temperatures and an increase in cloud cover. Rain possible."

Compare that brief description to one taken off the web during a typical day in July 2013 in the State of Virginia, the date of and location at which this article is being written:

> Widespread showers and thunderstorms developing by 1 PM. Mostly cloudy with temperatures in the low 80s. WSW winds shifting to N at 10 to 15 mph. Humidity steady at 74%. UV Index 5 to moderate. Pollen count low. Dew Point 72 degrees.

Visibility 10.0 miles. Sunrise 6:11 AM and sunset 8:43 PM. Moon phase is waxing crescent. Zero precipitation past 24-hours. Chance of rain 80%.

Not only is the report more detailed and informative, today weather forecasting is more than merely a declaration of existing and developing events. Much effort is being expended to better understand how the many components of weather, and their association with natural phenomena, relate to the economics, well-being and long-term aspects of humanity. Consider the numerous articles published almost daily regarding shifting oceanic currents and hurricane frequency, volcanic eruptions and pollution and the interplay of population growth and global warming, including even the denial of any effect from either. More specifically, and in a related context, consider the years of 1935 and 1936 in Shelby County.

It was a winter of extended despair. Temperatures began to fall around Christmas week, but by late January thermometers in exposed locations plunged to levels as low as 30 degrees below zero. Local records, a few dating back to 1879, were established at a level even old-timers had not experienced. Driven from the northwest by gale-force winds exceeding 35 miles per hour, the coldest wave reported to have hit the American midcontinent region in more than 15 years paralyzed the entire Buckeye State. Blizzard-force storms marked new records with snow accumulating into 20-foot drifts. School children were marooned in rural schools, and automobiles and trucks were stranded on both county roads and major highways.

Conditions continued for five consecutive days and nights across all of the eastern states. Eventually this weather event was declared the most intense since the turn of the century, exceeding even the memorable "winter of 1917." Frostbite and freezing temperatures took more than 100 lives. The mighty Niagara Falls even fell victim to huge ice jams.

After a brief respite from the bitter cold, a second and then a third wave enveloped the region. On February 18, 1936, the Weather Bureau announced, on the basis of information collected from throughout the Middle West, the previous 30 days had been the coldest in the history of record keeping. Traffic everywhere in the region was imperiled by Arctic gales, towns were increasingly isolated and food and fuel shortages developed on a daily basis.

By Tuesday the 25th, an ice jam extending over a distance of three miles was affecting the flow of the Great Miami River below and upstream to the B & O Railroad Bridge (today the CSX Railroad), south of Sidney. Rain that night only added to the problem, raising the level of the river 8.2 feet above normal. Estimated to be flowing at speeds of 10 to 12 miles per hour, the flood-swollen river created a serious problem in the Kirkwood-Lockington area as the dammed waters threatened the old covered bridge, an historic landmark of the vicinity.

The winter of 1935-1936 was certainly one for the record books, no doubt of that, but why did it take place? Was it a fluke of nature, one that had to make an appearance every now and then, or was there a rationale for its occurrence? Was it somehow related to an earlier phenomenon? If cold and snow were the effect, could there have been a related cause, and what might that cause be? If there were a cause, how might it be found and identified?

Presumably, the richest source of information about the record cold of '35-'36 in Shelby County can be found in the tucked-away, corner room on the basement level of the Amos Memorial Library, where multi-drawer cabinets filled with rolls and rolls of boxed and labeled microfilm are stored. Here, the thousands and thousands of pages that once made up the daily and weekly editions of Sidney's major newspapers -- the *Shelby County Democrat, The Sidney Journal* and the *Sidney Daily News* -- are available to anyone with the eyesight and patience to do the searching. For this particular task, that means reviewing the pages of newspaper editions published during the central years of the 1930s.

In Shelby County newspapers of that era, the significant, above-the-fold news of the day pertained principally to the continuing economic depression that began during the autumn of 1929. This information seemed irrelevant to the query at hand, for even a relatively uninformed person would quickly surmise there is a minimal relationship between economics and weather. Beyond the front pages, the occasional death and fire is mentioned, along with the even less occasional murder, if not in the city or county then elsewhere in the region, but human tragedies and assorted acts of mayhem do not relate well to the cycles of daily weather. In short, the records of the daily press appear to offer no clue at all.

But wait, let's go back to the *Sidney Daily News* edition of April Fools Day, 1936. There on an inside page is a 4 x 4.5 inch collage of photographs with an accompanying caption that within the space of six lines contains two intriguing phrases, one reading "dust bowl" and the other "black rollers." If there is a link between natural phenomena and weather, might this be it?

As the old saying goes: "politics may be local, but weather isn't." Upon return to my Virginia home, I turned to that modern-day technological wonder of fact, fiction and truth -- the world-wide-web. Once the phrase "weather phenomena" was fed into a favorite search engine, a plethora of information was delivered. The phrase "dirty thirties" jumped off the computer screen. Defined as a period of severe, dust-laden storms that caused major ecological and agricultural damage to American prairie lands in the 1930s, might these gigantic windstorms of swirling, microscopic particles also be related to the record-breaking Ohio and Shelby County winter of 1935-1936? Had I identified a "eureka moment?"

By the late 1800s, families intending to purchase and farm acreage sufficient to realize their dreams of security and happiness had widely settled the Great Plains. At that time, the land was clothed in Buffalo grass, a short, 8- to-10-inch high, naturally occurring plant that readily held moisture in the earth and kept the soil from desiccating and blowing away, even during periods of minimum rainfall. Within a few decades, however, farmers had ploughed and seeded much of this virgin soil, their principle crop being wheat. When the demand for wheat increased with the U. S. entry into World War I in 1917, the farming community reacted by ploughing even more grassland, a trend that continued even after the armistice. By 1930, a glut had developed in the wheat market, and prices began to fall.

One year later, a severe drought descended across the region, from Texas north to the Canadian border. Crops began to die and without natural anchors to hold the soil in place the over-ploughed land, taking on the appearance of a desert, dried, turned to dust and blew away, carried to the east by prevailing winds. Within the period of 12 months, the number of dust storms doubled, increasing from 14 to 28. In 1934, high-level winds carried a reported 350 million tons of dust from the northern Great Plains to the eastern seaboard and beyond. Ships 300 miles at sea in the Atlantic Ocean collected dust on their decks. The first of a series of "black rollers" was born on the 11th day of May and the worst was yet to come.

On Palm Sunday, April 14, 1935, folks living in the panhandle region of Oklahoma woke to a morning bathed by bright sunshine and calm winds. By 4:20 PM, however, afternoon brightness had turned to midnight darkness. The temperature plunged 40 degrees, and a 10,000-foot-high wall of dirt churned out of the north, carried by polar air currents originating in Canada. Visibility was reduced to zero, and residents were forced to crawl on hands and knees in search of shelter. On this day, forever known as "Black Sunday," a reporter trapped in his vehicle during the storm coined the phrase "dust bowl," a term that would soon become associated with destitute lifestyles and abandoned farmsteads. At the time, the subject of "dust," defined simply as fine, particulate matter, was of minimal interest to the scientific world. Its' history, however, when examined, became a matter of extreme concern.

Black Sunday in Texas.

In 1783 a massive column of poisonous ash rising from the erupting Laki volcano in Iceland spread over Europe within a matter of days. It lingered there for months, creating a hot summer, a very cold winter -- one of the worst on record -- and thousands of deaths. In the United States, the average winter temperature dropped some five degrees.

One century later, the explosion of Krakatoa in the East Indies sent a five-cubic-mile cloud of ash 25 miles into the stratosphere. Carried by the jet stream, it circled the world in two weeks, darkened the skies around the equator and within a year had caused a 2.2-degree decline in average global temperature. Temperatures did not return to normal until 1888.

In February 2013, a university study reported that one of the driest spots on Earth -- the Sahara Desert -- is increasingly responsible for snowfall half a world away in the western United States. Instruments mounted in aircraft flying in the skies over the Sierra Nevada Mountains detected minute particles that had originated in the arid Sahara. Analyses indicate these particles play a significant role in how efficiently clouds produce precipitation.

It has been known for a long time that storm-produced, wind-borne dust, carried high enough into the atmosphere, can be blown to various locations around the globe, all the time affecting local weather. The particles of dust stimulate the formation of ice crystals in clouds that, in turn, influence how much rain or snow falls in the region covered by the dust-laden cloud.

One particular study focused on two quite similar storms that occurred a week apart over eastern California. The first storm was relatively free of dust, whereas the second formed in clouds filled with dust. Snowfall associated with the second was 40% heavier than that derived from the first. Viewed from another perspective, atmospheric dust can filter the warming effects of sunshine and create a cooler environment. Airborne dust, therefore, appears to be an important element in the formation of both local and regional patterns of temperature and precipitation.

A detailed review of the microfilm newspaper records for the period 1934 into 1936, as preserved in the Amos Memorial Library, indicates that the occurrence of massive storms across the western landscapes of the United States -- those now identified with the "Dust Bowl" -- was a news item of minimal merit to Shelby County readers. These atmospheric disturbances devastated the prairie states of Texas, Oklahoma, Kansas, Nebraska and North and South Dakota and forced thousands of persons to leave their wasted lands and move to California-- a migration preserved in the pages of The Grapes of Wrath, the classic tale of dust and defeat written by John Steinbeck.

The roiling curtains of dust surely moved across the Buckeye State, but at an altitude that caused no immediate visual effect at the ground level. Those living in Shelby County eventually became conversant with the term "black rollers," but at the time they considered them an aspect of weather that was taking place "out west," and so not to worry. Their property and lifestyle were unaffected. They were right in their viewpoint, at least for a period of eight months, and then came the dawn of a new season and the winter of 1935-1936, with its record cold, deep drifting snow and back-to-back blizzards.

With the advantage of hindsight and advanced technology, might it now be said the record winter of '35 -'36 was caused by cold temperatures and massive storms triggered by the lingering affects of high-altitude clouds that crossed Ohio months before, pregnant with volumes of dust derived from the dehydrated soils of the prairie states? Information gleaned from the eruptions in Iceland and the East Indies and the heavy snowfalls of the Sierra Nevada Mountain province is evidence this question could very well be answered in the affirmative.

If so, Ohio did not, to use modern vernacular, "dodge the Dust Bowl bullet." It just took a few months for that atmospheric projectile to affect its weather and landscape. Of course, this hypothesis cannot be proven beyond a shadow of scientific doubt, but until there is better information, an effect and cause hypothesis cannot be dismissed. The Buckeye State and Shelby County may have spent the Dust Bowl years of 1934-1935 woefully unaware of what lay nascent, only to be affected by the aftermath of the dust storms during the winter of 1935-1936.

RECOLLECTIONS OF THIS AND THAT

That and this, this and that, mix them up, shuffle and reshuffle, discard and add and shuffle again and the result begins to resemble a potpourri. This fifth and final "chapter" of an encore history of Shelby County, is such a potpourri.

The first two accounts are recollections of a youth who, when he was not found at home or in school, was either free to roam through what was then known simply as "Tawawa Lake," or was expected to be involved in various church activities.

The final three narratives focus on an individual who for a period of 36 years -- 1869 to 1905 -- was considered by many the spirit and conscience of Sidney and Shelby County. As editor of *The Sidney Journal*, William Binkley never hesitated to use his position to persuade public opinion and prod public action. As a self-declared politician-without-portfolio, he continually fought, on the statewide level, any and all efforts to denigrate what he considered the high principles of the Republican Party. As an individual with an investigative bent he daily prowled the streets of the community in search of news and a good story.

At Binkley's retirement party, held at the Wagner Hotel in 1905, Judge Harrison Wilson characterized him as one who had fought for more good measures than any other editor in the State of Ohio, and "carried a good conscience into every column of your paper." On a more personal level, he praised Binkley for being "unlike the rich men who first made their millions, and then give them away, you would give yours away before you made them." He concluded the editor had gathered "here in this little city a colony of friends whose regard for you can not be excelled in the all the great metropolises of America."

TALES OF TAWAWA

Before 1948 the area was just another segment of East Sidney. Characterized by rolling and forested topography it was dominated by a lake that all the local lads knew had no bottom -- well, at least it had supposedly never been reached. A large boulder lay sheltered in a shaded glen further to the east, a creek named either "Mosquito" or "Tawawa" ran through the region and a "millrace" bordered by a "lovers' lane" meandered hither and yon. After the end of the Second World War it was rumored the land might be used for a housing development much needed by veterans returning from military service, but the circumstances were meant to be otherwise.

Approaching the Big Rock on a Sunday afternoon in the spring of 1948, Kenneth McDowell and Cecil Watkins were alerted to a noisy crowd of motorcyclists discussing the possibility of using the locale as a club rendezvous site. Alarmed, they shared ideas on the way home as to how the area might be preserved for future generations of Sidney residents.

In a matter of weeks the Tawawa Civic Park Association had been formed and a Board of Trustees named. The first order of business was the identification of 15 civic-minded citizens, each of whom might contribute $1,000 toward the purchase of a block of land that could form the core of the projected park. When Wendal E. Whipp, President of Monarch Machine Tool Company, was approached for his expected contribution, he magnanimously wrote a personal check for the entire amount with the suggestion: "go buy the land and then go to the others for their money and let's get this project started." One hundred and ten acres were initially purchased, and Tawawa Park was established. Deeded to the city in March of 1956, today its' 220 acres are treasured as Tawawa Civic Park, the crown jewel in the 16-park-system administered by the City of Sidney.

Thousands of persons take advantage of the varied park facilities on a seasonally adjusted basis: softball diamonds, soccer fields, fishing, sand volleyball, picnic areas and numerous areas set aside as open green space where nature can be experienced free of the clutter and noise of the city. There is more, however, to Tawawa than meets the eye -- the Tawawa of history and mystery. As a teen-ager, I spent many an adventuresome summer day probing the nooks and crannies of Tawawa, testing the outdoor skills I was learning as a member of Holy Angels Church Boy Scout Troop 95 or just letting my thoughts probe the wonders of Mother Nature.

At a moment's notice, I could leave my parents' home on East Court Street, walk to the top of Orbison Hill, turn north onto Foster Avenue to Feree Avenue and then follow a little-worn path that led to the slope overlooking the west side of the lake. It didn't take me long to make the trip, fifteen minutes or so and I was there. It took a bit longer, however, to arrive at answers to my inquiries about this region of nature, such as:

- ---Why is the park so hilly and downtown Sidney so flat?
- ---Was Lovers' Lane really constructed just for lovers?
- ---Why was the road though the area straight as an arrow and where did it go?
- ---Is Tawawa Lake natural or man-made?
- ---Where did the Big Rock come from and why are others not present?
- ---And, a mystery question -- does the park really have a World War II history?

PASSAGES

After many hours of searching old newspaper accounts and checking into a variety of reference books, I do believe I have a few answers.

THE HILLY AND FLAT QUESTION!

Tawawa Park is built on a foundation of solid rock deposited by a shallow sea that flooded western Ohio during the Silurian Period of geologic time, 443 to 416 million years ago. Towards the end of the Silurian Period, the entire state was uplifted by tectonic forces associated with the early construction of the Appalachian Mountains. Shelby County was elevated above sea level at that time and has remained so ever since.

Then less than 3 million years ago, temperatures declined in North America, frozen snow fields formed in Canada and massive tongues of glacial ice repeatedly invaded Ohio. The last encroachment occurred 25,000 years ago, spread across the landscape on average several hundred feet per year, reached its most southeasterly position and then began a final retreat to the north, melting back through Shelby County 20,000 to 18,000 years ago.

The ice left behind a terrain composed of silt, sand and boulders gouged from the landscape over which the ice had moved. In Shelby County this material averages 100 feet in thickness and forms distinctively different landscapes. To the west of the Great Miami River, there are four separate end moraines, linear ridges that represent periods of ice stagnation. To the east, the region that includes the Tawawa area, the glacial debris forms ground moraine, material similar to that found in end moraines but deposited with a more sporadic pattern. Bertsch Hill, Pointner Knoll and Wagner Glade are typical of the topographic features found there.

After the final tongue of glacial ice had retreated from Shelby County, the Great Miami River was established as a tributary to the Ohio River. During periods of flooding, the river meanders in a lateral direction, carving out an ever-expanding floodplain characterized by low relief. The end result of this extended span of geologic time is a half-mile wide flood plain upon which most of Sidney is built and an extensive field of ground moraine that forms the region of Tawawa Park.

What about Lovers' Lane?

A little research into old records suggests those individuals enthused with moments of romanticism favored a stroll along the millrace through Tawawa Park during the decades bracketing the beginning of the 20th century, but such was not the purpose behind its construction. In the years immediately following the Civil War the city of Sidney was faced with a dilemma – the means by which it was acquiring its' water supply had become antiquated. Townspeople were dependent on the water barrel, the cistern and the individual well for water for cooking, drinking, bathing and washing. Should a fire occur, the cry went out for formation of a fire-brigade system composed of a single individual managing a hand-operated pump and a line of volunteer, bucket passing citizens. An updated means of supplying water to home and community was needed.

Studies were conducted by geologists of the topography and natural sources of water, not only in Sidney but throughout many communities of western Ohio. The resulting report was most encouraging, as published in the December 16, 1870 issue of *The Sidney Journal*: "neighboring citizens . . . have not living springs upon adjoining heights (such as we do) which they can bring into town and elevate into the highest story of every building at a moderate expense." The springs that fed into Mosquito Creek were the recognized sources of water needed for the continued development of the community.

In order to channel the waters of Mosquito Creek into downtown Sidney, a millrace was dredged by a local contractor, beginning at a bend in the creek a mile or so east of the city and extending to a position along the east bank of the Great Miami River in Dingmansburg, today East Sidney. Millrace water would be collected in an 800,000-gallon capacity reservoir, fed through a water works building and then into the city through an underground field of metal pipes.

This cutting-edge water delivery system, completed in August of 1873, remained in operation until the late 1880s when a second-generation system, one relying on wells rather than surface water, was inaugurated. At that time the Mosquito Creek water source was abandoned, but the millrace through Tawawa Park remains largely intact to this day – and the path along its border is still available to strolling lovers.

Why the Straight Road through Tawawa Park?

In the late 1840s Sidney was a city with a bright future. Citizens anticipated the arrival of the Bellefontaine and Indiana Railroad, a major east-west rail system that would eventually link Indianapolis with Bellefontaine and the great market cities to the east. The connection, completed in June of 1853, ran through the heart of present-day Tawawa Civic Park, across the Great Miami River and through downtown Sidney, before exiting the corporation limits near what is today the intersection of Campbell Road and Interstate 75.

Over the years the line became associated with an increasing number of buggy, pedestrian and automobile accidents that took place at the numerous road crossings found within the community business sector. The problem grew in magnitude until the Flood of 1913 washed out large sections of the trackage. A decision was made by railroad officials to relocate the route to the south, crossing the river immediately north of the Graceland Cemetery by way of a projected, immense, five-arch, concrete structure that would soon be known as the "Big Four" bridge. The old downtown route was immediately abandoned, but the right-of-way through the woods of East Sidney remains, known today as Whipp Road. The old rail course was straight and thus Whipp Road is straight.

What is the Story of Tawawa Lake?

In order to maintain a near-horizontal roadbed during the construction of the Bellefontaine and Indiana Railroad any and all low-lying areas along the route had to be "filled in and smoothed out." In 1852, one such lowland was enclosed by a 1,300-foot-long embankment that formed a 50- to 60-foot-deep void along its' south side. Twenty years later, the millrace – a portion of a new water system mentioned above -- was dredged through the region, connecting the waters of Tawawa Creek with Sidney by way of the embankment void. Flowage through the millrace quickly filled in the topographic cavity, which then was named Tawawa Lake, in recognition of the source of the water.

What is the Origin of the Big Rock?

Ward Trail, the poorly defined path that exits Whipp Road east of Tawawa Lake, ends in a woodland glen filled with a gargantuan, rounded, 1,250-cubic-foot boulder estimated to weigh 103 tons. This artifact of nature – named Big Rock -- was identified in the early 1850s by workers constructing the right-of-way of the Bellefontaine and Indiana Railroad. Long considered a mystery wrapped within a shroud of confusion, the geology and derivation of Big Rock is now well documented.

Some three million years ago temperatures throughout North America began to decline, a climate signal that a new Ice Age was under way. Huge tongues of glacial ice, spawned by frozen snow fields located in central Canada, gradually flowed to the south, all the while absorbing fragments of the fractured bedrock over which it moved. Reaching a southerly point of advancement, the ice melted, leaving behind the captured remnants of rock. Big Rock is one such fragment.

The Big Rock of Tawawa Civic Park

Big Rock is a massive boulder of granite, a rock characterized by the presence of two common minerals, quartz and feldspar. The nearest source of granite to Shelby County is a 985-million-year-old geologic region of Canada that lies 150 miles to the north of Toronto. Years of study by geologists show this to be the home of the Tawawa giant. Quarried from the ancient basement of Canada by glacial ice, transported to the south and southwest over 700 miles and unceremoniously deposited in Shelby County, Big Rock remains an intriguing and demonstrative evidence of the mile-thick ice sheet that once enveloped Ohio in its chilling grip.

In 1936, Big Rock was officially dedicated as the "Council Rock of the Boy Scouts of Shelby County" during ceremonies conducted under the direction of the Shelby County Advisory Board. Following appropriate remarks regarding the history of the rock, members from all six county scout troops "assembled around the huge camp fire," sang the Scout Vesper song and stood at attention as Taps were played.

WHAT IS THE RELATIONSHIP OF TAWAWA CIVIC PARK TO EVENTS OF WORLD WAR II?

In 2011 the eastern limits of the park were extended by the addition of the Brookside parcel, a plot of land formerly used as a campsite by the local Girl Scout organization. Many years before, during World War II, the same land was used as the site of a shooting range by members of the local National Guard attachment and by members of various Regular Army units stationed at Patterson Air Field in Dayton.

In late September of 1943, the 240-soldier-strong 407th Air Service Squadron arrived at the site, quickly dubbed Camp Swezey, for training in military field maneuvers and firearms practice. The first all Chinese-American unit accepted into the roll call of the U. S. Army, the 407th was destined for eventual service in China as a member of the 14th Air Force -- the infamous "Flying Tigers." Their week long stint at Camp Swezey was but one of several instances when present-day Tawawa land was employed as a training ground for men who would be engaged overseas during World War II in the fight for democracy.

Two months earlier, residents of East Sidney were suddenly startled by the sight of a "heavy bomber zooming towards the ground . . . its motors spitting and coughing alarmingly . . . followed by a loud crash in the Tawawa Lake vicinity." Flying at an altitude of 27,000 feet, the four-engine military craft was returning to its home base in Dayton when "a super-charger failed and knocked out one of its four motors. A propeller and part of the motor's cowling were hurled loose and sent earthward . . . the plane lost considerable altitude and roared low over treetops and houses." The propeller was found "deeply embedded in the ground near the lake" several hours after the experimental aircraft had "limped safely into Wright field on three motors." This incident remains perhaps the only time that any damage was inflicted on Shelby County by events associated with World War II.

Today thousands of residents annually enjoy the many attributes of Tawawa Civic Park, but a majority of these individuals remain oblivious to the storied facets of this rustic realm of nature. Endowed with a richness of fact and history these Tales of Tawawa remain a treasure silently waiting discovery by those who display any degree of interest and curiosity.

OLD TIME RELIGION

The gathering clouds of change coalesced into a full thunderhead of transformation on the 11th of October 1962 when the opening session of the Second Vatican Council was solemnly called to order. More than 2,500 elaborately robed leaders assembled in the concourse of St. Peter's Basilica in a massive display of solemn ecclesiastical pomp that has since become known as Vatican II. As soon as the requisite Mass had ended with the traditional blessing of the congregation, Pope John XXIII took to the pulpit and reiterated his intent in calling the Council into session, the first since the great congregation of 1870: "It was time to open the windows and let in some fresh air." For many Catholics, laymen and clergy alike -- and especially those of a traditionalist bent -- the air came in at gale force.

The changes accomplished by the Second Vatican Council, which concluded on December 7, 1965, the day of the Feast of the Immaculate Conception, were in liturgy, administrative practices and, of greatest importance, ecumenism. Questions arose and were answered on: the position of the altar, tabernacle and baptistery; the alignment of pews, statues and candles, windows and walls, aisles and entrances; and the location of the baptismal font. The guidelines made the process somewhat simple: "Nothing cheap, trivial, pretentious or superficial should be used."

To achieve this grand purpose, Pope John listed several aims of the

Council: the bishops and priests must grow in holiness, the laity must be given effective instruction in Christian faith and morals, an adequate provision must be made for the education of children, and Christian social activity must increase.

Priests began to celebrate the Mass in the vernacular, instead of in Latin, and were positioned to face the congregation, a signal the worshippers were a vital part of the service. Communion was to be taken by the hand, rather than by the tongue, and abstinence from meat on Friday was no longer widely practiced. Nuns discarded their order-distinctive habits in favor of civilian styles and were encouraged to take on popular causes such as those of civil and workers' rights. In short, the "open window" policy re-defined the Catholic Church as "its people," not its buildings and cumbersome altars and tabernacles, and called upon those people to be active rather than passive participants in the practices of their religion.

Over the years, the changes manifested themselves in many ways. Weekly Mass participation began to deteriorate, as did the need to periodically participate in the Sacrament of Confession. Holy day attendance seemed no longer of importance and dress codes used for Mass slowly altered from the formal to those viewed as ordinary and lax. The Pope had expressed the mission of Vatican II in one of his favorite Italian words -- "aggiornamento" -- meaning the Church must adapt itself to meet the challenging conditions of modern times.

By the time the variances of Vatican II had reached the sacristy of Holy Angels Church in Sidney, I had left my parents' home on East Court Street, gained an education, married and moved to California. I was far too busy with career and family to notice the ways and means in which the Mass was now being conducted during my Sunday attendances. Over the next half dozen or so decades of time, other interests and attractions caught my attention. I accepted the new environment of my church without question, caught up in the normal process of living. Now, in a stage of life best defined as post-maturity and pre-dotage, I have cause to reflect upon those pre-Vatican II years during which I grew to maturity, everlastingly influenced by family, community and, of specific importance, the presence of the Gothic-style building that defines the corner of South Main Avenue and East Water Street.

Holy Angels Church was consecrated on Sunday, May 15, 1892, by Archbishop William H. Elder of Cincinnati. Built at a cost of $41,000 on land deeded to the parish trustees by Ida Dickas, wife of Christopher Heinrich Dickas, its two near-identical towers reached heights of 165 and 115 feet. A reported one million bricks were used in its construction, and 800 people could be comfortably seated within its exterior dimensions of 60 by 140 feet. The interior was cruciform in shape, with the central aisle representing the beam of the cross and the transept the arms. The altar, constructed of white walnut inlaid with gold leaf, occupied an alcove in the north end and was graced by enveloping paintings, the one to the east depicting the death of St. Joseph and the other to the west showing the first meeting of the Holy Family after Christ had risen from the dead.

Light cascading through nearly 40 windows, constructed of the finest cathedral stained glass, lit up the interior with a spectrum of color. The parish planning committee and contract architect choose two of these, circular in design, to depict Cherubim, the celebrated second order of angels, to give rationale to the official name, The Church of the Holy Angels. Today, these celestial visitors continue to look down in encouragement and approval upon the worshipers.

This is the church in which I, along with 45 classmates, received First Communion on May 4, 1941, and in which 18 days later I received the Sacrament of Confirmation. It was there that I participated in Profession of Faith ceremonies, in May of 1947, and seven months later was inducted into The Sodality of Our Blessed Lady, a status that entitled me "to all the indulgences, favors, graces and privileges which other Sodalists enjoy." The solemn rituals of Pentecost, Advent, Lent and Epiphany and the anticipation of the joyful seasons of Easter and Christmas also punctuated those growing-up years. May Day, the celebration of the Virgin Mary, the Mother of God, the ringing of the Angelus three times each day, at 6 AM, Noon and 6 PM, the sadness of Good Friday and standing in line for weekly Confession defined my early life as a Catholic as well.

In those pre-Vatican II days, parochial education during the academic year began with daily Mass. Holy Angels Church is of the size that all 12 grades could simultaneously occupy the central two-thirds of the configuration of oaken pews. As pliant first graders, we sat and knelt in the front several rows below the Communion railing and to the right of the close-by main alter. With the passage of years our class position was changed by zig-zag movement back and forth across the central isle until finally, as exalted seniors, we occupied the last several rows of pews in the very back of the church, facing the left side of the distant altar.

There, for some 190 early morning weekdays of each academic year, we participated in the "Holy Sacrifice of the Mass." Attentiveness was the exact order of the day. Should we squirm, be caught chewing gum or misbehave in any manner commonly associated with adolescents, a presiding nun delivered in a loud whisper an instant reminder that if we did not cease and desist the immediate hell-fires of retribution would descend upon us with decided emphasis.

During the years immediately prior to and following the time of World War II, the 16 girls and 14 boys who made up the Holy Angels graduating class of 1951 were academic lieges to a devoted community of women who lived their daily lives enveloped in head-covering, rolled wimples attached to starched white and circular dickeys and robes of black wool cinched with waist-circling, three-foot-long rosaries that gave each nun an aura of unquestioned authority. Sister Reinette Marie began the process of instruction and education in 1939, and when her responsibilities were completed we were graduated to the next of a series of Sisters of Charity of Cincinnati: Eileen Therese, Agnes Mary, Ann Xavier, Mary Thomas, Mary Elizabeth, Ann Simion and Catherine Seton. Sisters Mary Sylvia, Kathleen Mariam, Agnes Ellen and Marie Devota conducted the high school curriculum. Sister Esther occupied the front office as principal and helped when needed in the duties of two nuns-at-large: Joseph Mary who directed business courses and Mary Augusta who wielded the baton in all matters of music. Through it all, we experienced 12 years in the same church and school and were served with 12 only slightly different versions of the same faith -- Catholicism.

Somewhere around 1944, I became an altar boy, the attendant to the presiding priest during the liturgical service of Mass. From the viewpoint of ritual and occasion, three Mass versions were available to the faithful. The Solemn Mass was performed rarely, and involved extensive, incense-laden ceremonies in which the presiding priest, robed in vestments proper for the occasion, was assisted by a deacon, sub-deacon, a choir and as many servers as were necessary. These Masses were the occasion of major feast days and visits by Church dignitaries.

Low Mass, the most common form of Mass, was an abridgement of the "Solemn" ceremony, in which the priest, generally assisted by two servers, assumed the duties of deacon and sub-deacon and a choir was absent. Weekday Mass was of this nature.

High Mass was intermediate in design and ritual and was really "Low" in nature. It was, however, beautified with chants, psalm and melodies, in which the entire congregation could participate. Incense was used on occasion. Generally, four servers assisted in the ceremony. During the years of World War II, the Sunday services at Holy Angels Church consisted of one High Mass, generally performed at 10 AM, and as many as four Low Masses, the first beginning at 6 AM and the last ending around 12:30 PM.

As presented by Sister "Agie" Allen the learning process of becoming a bona fide altar boy involved two fields of understanding: (1) how to act and move, and (2) when and what to say. With great patience, she introduced each step, repetition upon repetition, until the choreography gelled into a concert of graceful and memorized steps. The first half of the Mass consisted of 11 movements, ranging from the prayers at the foot of the altar through the Creed and the profession of Catholic faith. The concluding half was composed of the Offering, the Consecration and the Communion.

Through the entire ritual, ranging anywhere from 30 minutes for the "Low" version to an hour or more in length for the "High" version, the Mass slowly unfolded. As a server, I was taught to move about the altar with assurance, kneel with composure, eyes forward and back erect, palms flat and fingers touching as in prayer. Always maintain the dignity of the moment, never yielding to a sneeze, an errant itch, or the buzzing of a fly. Street clothes were to be covered by a full-length black, and constantly in-need-of-dry-cleaning cassock topped by a white surplice, and pity the lad who showed up in a pair of gym shoes.

The Mass dialogue was delivered in Latin by the priest and answered by the server in words of proper response:

> "*In nomine Patris, et Filii et Spiritus Sancti.*" (In the name of the Father, the Son and the Holy Spirit).
>
> "*Ad Deum qui laetificat juventutem mean.*" (To God who giveth joy to my youth).
>
> "*Kyrie eleison, Christie eleison, Kyrie eleison.*" (Lord have mercy, Christ have mercy, Lord have mercy).

Even the Low Mass was imbedded with subtle actions. Ring the hand-held bells three times during the Consecration of the Communion wafer and three times during the offering of the wine, but immediately prior to the second ring of each sequence reach out and grasp the priest's chasuble so it would not touch the floor during his act of kneeling. And, should at any time it be necessary to cross the altar, pause at mid-point and genuflect, upon one knee for a Low Mass and upon both for the High Mass version.

Along with my fellow servers, I took assigned turns for these duties for more than four years, commonly assisting either Father James Dossman, Father James Peaker or Monsignor Edward Lehman at the 6 AM weekday Mass. The task completed, I returned home, ate breakfast and then joined my classmates for the ritual school day service. I have no idea how many Mass attendances I accumulated over the years, but in 1948 I was awarded the Ad Altare Dei medal, a Boy Scouts of America recognition that in those pre-Vatican II days could be earned only after serving a minimum of 250 hours as an altar boy.

Catholics who came of age in the middle of the 20th century are acutely aware of the appeals of Christ for devotion to His philosophy as manifested by the reception of Holy Communion on nine successive First Fridays' of the Month. The purpose of this practice was reparation for committed offences, and the rewards for those who persevered month after month were believed to be beyond earthly purchase: peace in their homes, solace in their labors and comfort in their afflictions. The greatest First Friday award of all, however, was the promise one would not die "in His disgrace or without the sacraments."

A second ritual that rolled around on a periodic basis was that of "Forty Hours" devotion, the time during which the Blessed Sacrament was displayed on the altar in memory of the same number of hours the body of God the Son remained in the sepulcher. The usual practice was for one to participate for 30 to 60 minutes in prayer repeatedly reciting the Our Father and Hail Mary prayers. Those who added an additional set of prayers for the reigning Holy Father received an "indulgence," defined as the remission of temporal punishment due for sin after the guilt has been forgiven. With my now-and-then involvement in the Stations of the Cross -- the religious enactment of the journey of Christ to Calvary Hill -- and participation in a funeral or wedding, my youthful presence at Holy Angels Church was frequent and expected.

This was the Holy Angels Catholic Church of the mid-20th century -- before Vatican II. The church year moved from one stage to the next with practiced regularity, the sacraments were to be observed whenever possible, the interpretations and dictates of the resident priests were beyond question and children were preferably raised in an environment administered through the cooperative actions of parents, priests and nuns. The religion of my youth was one of pomp, certainty, discipline and predictable reward.

And then, Pope John XXIII opened the windows and "let in some fresh air." The new Vatican II religion, considered by many Catholics, and most church leaders, as a step in the direction of progress, is succinctly exemplified by the words of Lance Morrow, American journalist and essayist: "Vatican II was a force that seized the mind of the Roman Catholic Church and carried it across the centuries from the 13th to the 20th."

To those Catholics who feel otherwise, the words of Jay P. Dolan, Professor Emeritus of History at Notre Dame University and a man widely known as the "master historian of Catholicism in America," ring with clarifying tones of veracity:

Before Vatican II, Catholics were struggling with the question of what it meant to be an American; comfortably American after Vatican II, they now struggled with a more fundamental question: what it meant to be a Catholic.

To this day, the question remains unsolved. It should be acknowledged, however, that for more than a few of the faithful, the "Old Time Religion" of the pre-Vatican II era was not necessarily considered outdated. The recollection of its' basic tenants, as practiced in Holy Angels Church during my 18 years of growing to maturity in Sidney, remain with me like the memory of many a person's proverbial childhood blanket: warm and fuzzy.

BLACK FRIDAY 1893

Designed and composed by William Binkley, co-owner and editor of *The Sidney Journal*, it was, by his own admission, the weekly newspaper's "first effort in the line of an illustrated trade issue." Published in a format of multiple subheads and exhortations and complete with beautifully executed photographic and lithographic visuals, readers were reminded to "judge of the expense attached" and note particularly the absence of "swell head write-ups designed to especially benefit personal interests." With confidence born of the enthusiasms of the day, Binkley concluded the editorial preamble to the Industrial Edition by stating the purpose of publication was "To show that the past prosperity and present accelerated progression are but the inevitable result of natural causes."

The date was February 10, 1893, and "The Gilded Age," an era defined by both unprecedented economic growth and grinding immigrant poverty, was entering its third decade of existence. Characterized by the rapid expansion of the domestic railroad network, the introduction of the factory system and accelerated increases in labor union membership, the value of the U. S. economy rose at the fastest rate in its history, as evidenced by rapid increases in wages, wealth and Gross Domestic Product.

The pages of the "Four Hundred," the ever-changing catalogue of the socially elite that represented the epitome of east coast society, were highlighted by the names of J. D. Rockefeller, Andrew W. Mellon,

Cornelius Vanderbilt and J. P. Morgan. Everyday miseries continued for those confined to the lower class, but for persons associated with the rising middle class life was better than it had ever been. For the small percentage of individuals whose mere existence gave definition to fashionable society life was – well, truly gilded.

One day short of two weeks later, the Philadelphia and Reading Railroad declared bankruptcy, the result of having overextended itself in a race to transportation supremacy. Almost simultaneously, recently opened mines flooded the market with silver, causing precious metal prices to drop and cotton and wheat farmers struggled under a parallel decline in crop values. Fearing the worst, people rushed to the banks to withdraw their savings and a credit crunch rippled through the American economy. The Panic of 1893 was under way.

Nine months later, as the holiday season approached, economic conditions had not improved all that much and the merchants and entrepreneurs of Sidney were, like those throughout America, uncommonly worried. After all, a significant portion of their annual income was usually realized during the month of December. During his daily wanderings around the square, William Binkley had little trouble sensing the pungent whiff of fear and concern that filled the storefronts and upon return to his office came up with a plan of action. The result, published on December 1, was certainly unusual: an abbreviated introduction to a small group of businessmen who, in all probability, had paid *The Sidney Journal* for advertising that was cleverly couched in terms that would hopefully greatly enhance holiday sales. Since *The Journal* published only on the sixth day of the week and the purpose was improvement in holiday shopping, this extended review could well be considered the very first example of "Black Friday" advertising to appear in any Ohio newspaper, or perhaps, any newspaper published anywhere in the United States.

Present-day consumers readily recognize the significance of the term "Black Friday," the right-of-passage event that annually signals the beginning of the traditional holiday shopping season. On this day immediately following Thanksgiving Day many merchants open their stores early in anticipation of the arrival of hordes of shoppers drawn by the advertising of special, limited time sales. The term was supposedly first used in the Philadelphia retail trade market in the early 1960s to describe the irksome pedestrian and vehicle traffic environment that traditionally occurred the day following Thanksgiving. To many merchants, however, the term indicates that time in the year in which they begin to make a profit on sales, that is, they begin to operate "in the black."

William Binkley died more than three decades before Black Friday became a recognized holiday shopping phenomenon in America, but the wording and format of the special merchant review as published in *The Sidney Journal* issue of Friday, December 1, 1893 is indicative he was very much aware of the importance of value-driven, holiday-shopping advertising. He never used the term Black Friday, but his purpose and intent in publishing an introduction to leading Sidney businessmen was in absolute harmony with the sense of the term as employed in modern-day advertising.

The headline to the 1893 review crowns an extended one-paragraph long introduction that readily establishes Sidney as an exceptional and enterprising, mid-western, up-and-coming community ready, willing and indeed eager to embrace the opportunities of the approaching 20th century. Enthusiastic introductions to the owners of fourteen leading community businesses followed -- of which ten are chosen for repetition here in abbreviated form:

FACTS WORTH KNOWING ABOUT SIDNEY

Sidney is one of the best points for business of any town in the State of a relative size. It is the center of a large, thickly settled and wealthy agriculture district, unsurpassed by any in the Union. A glance at our densely packed business thoroughfares on an average day will speedily convince the most skeptical that as a trading center it has no superior. People from far beyond the bounds of Shelby county come here to lay in their supplies, a fact which is creditable to the tact, energy and enterprise of our merchants, who can compete in every line with those of Dayton, Cincinnati and other large cities in the State, and, in fact, in many branches are much below their rates. This they are enabled to do because all running expenses are lighter, rents and taxes are lower, help cheaper, cost of living less, beside other advantages in their favor. The readers of *The Journal* who live here and enjoy the advantages of our institutions, and the patronage of the people of this locality should use every means to further their interests as a whole, as well as their own, by patronizing home industry. The holidays are rapidly approaching and we are aware that many are of the opinion that desirable articles can not be purchased here. This is a mistake. Give your home merchant a chance, and if what you want is not kept in stock he will gladly send and get it for you, and at as low, if not lower, figure than you would pay otherwise. Do not visit other places to buy goods. You are doing Sidney and its business men an injustice. Our business men are wide awake, and when making purchases procure as many bargains as the merchants of other towns and they never fail to give their patrons the benefits. Sidney merchants always treat their customers and visitors courteously, and make friends with everybody. If you have been in the habit of buying elsewhere, resolve to stop it at once, and go out, inspect the stocks and hear the prices quoted. Their facilities for doing business are not exceeded by those of any place, and they will be found strictly trustworthy and worthy of all patronage extended to them.

I. H. THEDIECK

Everybody in Shelby county and thousands outside of it are familiar with the name Thedieck, which for years has been inseparably connected with the dry goods trade of this region. Last Saturday and all of this week there had been a crush at Mr. Thedieck's store, which is doing as large, if not larger, business than ever. This statement to some may sound extraordinary in view of the recent business depression, but a few days ago, when a *Journal* representative called, Mr. Thedieck smiled, and said the people of Shelby county always would buy where they found what they wanted and at their prices. He is offering great bargains in every department of his immense establishment, which is attracting hundreds every day. Then, again, he is pushing his business and letting the people know that he bought cheaper, and can in consequence sell cheaper. He bought for cash instead of credit, which has given him a great advantage. This fall, Mr.

Thedieck made a solemn resolve first he would sell everything cheaper than he ever has before, and, beside, give each and every customer a silverware ticket. If you do not believe he is keeping his resolution, join the crowds daily visiting his store and see for yourself. You will be interested, even if you do not purchase.

SHOES! SHOES!

In this day of polished shoes and dainty gaiters, people take care that they wear articles which are shapely and stylish. They do not forget comfort altogether, as of yore. Knowing these things, W. J. Kinstle, who a month ago opened the City Shoe Store in the Johnston room, East side square, has already made himself famous because he has been able to please the public to a greater extent in quality and prices than any other house which ever had inception here.

A BUSY STORE

One of the finest, most attractive as well as one of the busiest, stores of Sidney which we frequently have occasion to visit is that of Piper Brothers, who unquestionably carry one of the finest selected stocks of fancy and staple groceries in the city. These men started this business with the firm conviction that the people of Shelby county want the best and purest goods, and judging from the large and influential trade which they control, there can be no possible doubt but what they were correct.

WELL DRESSED MEN

The men of Sidney, that is, the most of them, are noted for their neat, trim and well- dressed appearance. This is especially true of those who patronize the fine merchant tailoring establishment of A. Mayer, located on the southwest corner of the square. His prices always were reasonable, and this season, on account of the recent financial difficulties, has laid in a larger stock than ever before, because he bought goods cheap, and is, therefore, enabled to offer great inducements.

DAZZLING IS THE DISPLAY

Wednesday we had occasion to drop into E. E. Kah's model store, and up to which time little thought had been given to the rapidly approaching holidays. Once you enter there you will realize they are close at hand. In the jewelry department he has an immense variety of pretty things...all the latest designs and novelties in jewelry, art pottery, fancy clocks, solid and plated silverware, also diamonds of the purest water, solid gold watches and everything in this line one could desire.

THE MUSIC TRADE

The increase in wealth and population in and around our city had developed a corresponding desire for all kinds of articles which minister to the comfort and pleasures of mankind. Particularly is this noticeable in the great demand which has arisen for pianos and organs, a demand which is well met by A. P. Shoaff, who conducts the leading music emporium of this region, and is doing a flourishing trade, but then, why should this not be the case? Through close business connections with the manufacturers he can offer inducements which few can equal.

BRIGHT IDEAS

In the days of ideas it requires a good one to attract attention, and as the ideas of H. Young, Bro. & Co. always keep trade flowing through the doors of their store, it is fair to suppose that their ideas must be exceptional. Last Saturday was the first day of their colossal green ticket sale, and it was, indeed, really surprising the way men's and boys' suits, overcoats and all the haberdashery a male human being needs nowadays disappeared from their store, and it is gratifying for *The Journal* to be able to state that, despite the cry on every side of hard times, the prosperity of their model, one price establishment has steadily advanced undisturbed by financial stringency or troubles.

AN ADVANCING ART

A visit a few days ago to the well known photograph gallery of C. W. VanDegrift has fully convinced the *Journal* representative that in no branch of the arts has more advancement been made in recent years than in that of photography. Mr. VanDegrift is one of the up to date photographers, who has kept pace with all the discoveries and improvements in the art. Beside photography, he has won an enviable reputation as an artist in crayon, ink and water colors, and his splendid artistic efforts can not be too highly commended.

A DRIVE IN FURNITURE

This is the season of the year when thoughts turn to winter comfort, likewise to the holidays, and, as people in general have a liking for fine furniture, it is pleasant to visit a house as that conducted by Marion O. Proctor, who about one month ago succeeded to the business conducted by Shaw Brothers. Never in the history of the furniture trade has there been more beautiful or more exquisite designs produced, and never has there been such an exhibit made in Sidney as that now on display at Mr. Proctor's, and which every resident of this community should see.

THE ARCADE

If you reside in the city or the country, or if you are a stranger, it will pay you to visit the Arcade, because it is actually a World's Fair in miniature, and you can spend several hours in good advantage looking over the many useful and curious articles which are there carried. To enumerate all would about fill *The Journal*, but suffice it to say that there is china, crockery and glassware from the leading manufacturers of France, Germany, England and America. Visit this establishment and look it over. It will be to your advantage, because the Messrs. Wagner acknowledge that never since starting business have they had such an immense stock in every department.

Was this review tainted by hype, exaggeration, embellishment, hyperbole and overstatement? Most certainly, it has it all, but then the holidays of 1893 were rapidly approaching and Sidney merchants were antsy to fill the drawers of their registers with hard cash, both green and silver in color. What better way than for *The Sidney Journal* to publish a paid advertisement featuring those businesses prepared to welcome the holiday shopper with bargain and choice. It was a win-win for newspaper and merchant alike and in the process William Binkley just might be credited with formulating the very first Black Friday sales event in the merchandizing history of America.

PERSONS ONCE REMEMBERED

In 1892, William Binkley, editor of *The Sidney Journal*, posted a succinct and quaint roll call of fondly remembered Shelby County men who had died during the two dozen or so years that had elapsed since the end of the Civil War. It remains today a listing of those persons who, in one fashion or another, contributed to the growth and history of Sidney and the surrounding area. Unusual in style and wording, it is presented here exactly as it was published on the front page of the May 27th issue, except that the names are in a different font for the convenience of contemporary readers.

As in most such writing during this time, the list does not include the many women in the area whose accomplishments and contributions were also important, but generally not acknowledged.

IN KINDLY REMEMBRANCE

Recollections of Those Who Have Passed Away --
Tersely Stated Characteristics

Still rolls the throng along our streets as of old, but forms and faces are missed, there are sounds of other footsteps than their own, they moved silently aside, their places are seemingly filled, and only in memory can we repeople our streets with those whom once we knew. May they not be entirely forgotten.

In the last quarter of a century how many familiar faces have vanished! Old friends who walked with us, old friends who talked with us, forever silent under the silencing sod. A mention of a few of their names may awaken many recollections.

Among the preachers who have died in the last 25 years we recall Kennedy, endeared to all our people; the gifted Armstrong; Spence, crowned with many years and the reverence of all; David Bulle, earnest in his work; P. A. Ogden, still revered; Jacob Weaver, unpretentious, but strong in the service, and the Rev. Alderman, still beloved by his old flock; the Rev. Hiram Shaull, a fervent apostle in the German Reformed church.

In the legal list are such names as Judge Conklin, brusque and forcible; John E. Cummins, strongly at the front; Edmund Smith, whose words had the emphasis of law; T. J. Petit, of poetic tendencies; W. J. Martin, quietly methodic; George M. Thompson, with a future of brilliant promise; T. J. McSweeney, quiet, but learned; James Murray, of high distinction; the gifted N. R. Burress; Bailey Walker, humorous and erudite; Judge Hugh Thompson, venerated by all our people; H. H. Sprague, whose mind went out in darkness so unfortunately; C. F. Yakey, successful in his pursuit; John McCullough, called away in his prime; the lovable student, Eddie Conklin; John H. Mathers, full of legal lore.

Here the list grows! There was Clay R. Joslin, whose ringing laugh will ever be missed; Thomas McCune, peace to his soul; Uncle William Skillen, full of humor; Judge N. R. Wyman, slight, but whose words had weight; David W. Pampel, whose deplorable death caused a universal heartache; H. A. Rhodehamel, the large hearted Gus; James H. Zinn, who died too soon, and Elijah Zinn, his father, quiet and full of business; E. M. Green, prominent in politics, and his son Fred, an exemplary young man; William Skidmore, strong in argument; D. V. Dingman, generous and unfortunate; B. W. Maxwell, pushing and thrifty; J. F. Frazer, constant to his business and his friends; G. H. Bunnelle whom Sidney will not cease to mourn; A. J. Robertson a man of gentlest temper, with a devotion to his home and his town.

How easy is it to recall David McCabe, honest, upright and true to all men; John Wagner, slow in speech, but always to the point; Enos Johnston, the genial Ene; James Irwin, lame, but sure; Samuel Lamb, with a good word for every body; John Clarey, always industrious; N. Levi, jolly and good natured; Ira Peebles, unpresuming, but true to his friends, and Abraham Clawson, the historian of early Sidney history.

Without effort comes to mind the memory of William C. Allen, for years the foreman of the *Journal* office; Charles Anderson, cut off in the midst of his business success; Ben. W. McCullough, of railway fame; J. S. Van Valkenburgh, the lively editor of the *Democrat*; George Leckey, whom the school children loved; S. A. Leckey, prominent in the interests of Sidney; E. Burnett, who revolutionized the hotel business here and elsewhere; Mathias Wagner, industrious and successful; Samuel Mathers, our old Postmaster, of quiet demeanor, father of Joe; C. I. Lewis, a stirring landlord of the Burnett House, and Frank Elliott and Father Stewart, whose love for little children was proverbial; David Edgar; James A. Wells, who kept the town straight -- by surveying; Ferdinand Amann, quiet in his habits and honest in his dealings with all men; George L. Bush, a man of the kindliest Christian character; Thomas Rank, who had carved the names of many, and another carved his; Dennis Mulvihill, who was Clerk of the Court and a droll boy; Fred Dickas, a promising boy who met his death by a runaway accident.

An ambitious student was John W. D. Wyman; Billy Ryan was an honest fisherman and never told a lie; John J. Skillen was making his mark as a business man when called away; John Baily is remembered in connection with the Bee Line; Uncle John Cashen celebrated the writer's birthday and St. Patrick's Day by being ground up by the cars. He was a jolly Irishman. A. M Weaver was our city surveyor, and an enthusiastic fisherman; John Sinks was a well known resident of the east side of the square, and a worthy man; Almon Hitchcock brought the New England energy with him to Sidney; Reuben Pepper was just making his mark in business, and L. C. Barkdull had made his, when death called them away. We remember John W. Carey, the banker, quick and business like, the progenitor of a busy family; who will forget John Morton, with all his genial qualities? Thomas Stephenson's memory is fresh with us all, old as he was; James Anderson was a well remembered clerk at the Burnett House; John Patton was one of the quietest of our residents and trustworthy, and R. Patton, once our gunsmith, lost his life by a mine explosion in the Far West; Isaac Bartholomew, one of our old residents, was killed by the cars at Piqua a short time after he got out of the sight of the writer; Joseph Brown was the victim of the insatiable cars in the West, and is buried here; Gottleib Lawrence was buried in a well across the river. We remember him as one of the quietest of men. Jacob Ziegler was a man of the highest commercial education, thorough in English and in German, and prospering.

Jeremiah Carey stands out in full view to the memories of all as a droll humorist, who allowed men to go to the barrel and fill their own tobacco boxes. We sadly miss Jerry. J. Q. A. Hertstein, who recently died, will be remembered through many a wedding suit in Sidney, though well worn; Michael Smith was a soft-hearted man in a hard iron business; James Wilkin was a painstaking, quiet carpenter, who said little and did a great deal; Robert L. Fry was once a familiar figure at the old corner. The sign is long since down. Samuel McCullough ended a long and busy life, which Sidney will long miss; Daniel Yohe raised half of Sidney -- on his flour; Fielding Dye was an honest farmer, moved to the city. He was a delightful delineator of times that reach clear back to the Indians.

We recall John Guy, the pioneer of the Baptist congregation here in Sidney, a wagonmaker who put wheels to the movement; Thomas B. Dunnavant, the tailor, strong in political argument; James Stephens, a prominent singer here in 1868, drowned in Illinois; William Cromer, who went through all the changes of fortune in Sidney to die by a railway accident, and John, his son, met an untimely death at the Dayton and Michigan railway hill; Aaron Brooks was small, but he is missed; Freeman Brooks, the livery stable keeper in Ohio street died some years ago; Samuel Rice was a quiet, retired farmer, and loved to live in Sidney; Benjamin Goode was well up in the literature of the day, with decided views.

We remember that Martin Chambers was an interesting talker, and we used to love to listen to his stories of old times; David Curtis never said much, but it always had the Irish point to it; G. S. Everett filed saws and was full of old saws -- a reasoning man; Eayre Haines was an unassuming, sensible man, an industrious worker all his life; Alfred Coon died in the West. He had a light-hearted soul that certainly needed no wings; Joseph Elliot used to help us hunt mushrooms -- a kindly spirit; J. L. VanGorder, killed by his horse; John Bushwaw, always at work; Lewis Boyer, vigorous and strong; Jacob Harmon, always with a pleasant word; E. J. Bayly, who enjoyed fishing and was an expert; William Berkshire, only lately laid away; Philip Montanus, an enthusiastic angler; Jacob Fraker, Robert Young, John Brubaker, John Clauson, all good residents.

Many of our musicians are gone. We remember Herman Tappe, leader of a successful Sidney band; Henry Heineman, a skilled musician; William Wycoff, whose life ended too soon; George Eddy who jarred his own life's strain; Frank Cleckner, a most worthy boy; William Rebstock and Louis Root, most justly mourned; Louis and Charles Nessler, both musicians; Eddy Thorn and Charlie Hale, cousins, and well liked by all.

The medical profession has also sustained losses. Among them we recall Dr. Henry S. Conklin, who gave to it two boys, one of them, Harry, dying at the beginning of a useful life; J. V. Lewis; Dr. Hare, who kept the drug store where the fruit store now is; Dr. Johnston, of many years' experience; Dr. Talbott, recently deceased, and Dr. Lefevre, who lately died in Georgia; Dr. Fielding, who served his patients and his State; Dr. Wood, who met his death in a runaway accident.

Among the younger lives that might have been spared to be a benefit to the town we might mention the names of Webster Kelsey, Eddie Timeus, Frank Amann, George Kah, Daniel Sollenberger, Aloys Wagner, Romy and Wyman Hill, brothers; James McCullough,

John Eisenstein, D. C. Hailman, Joseph Conklin, George Bayly, Alvin Weaver, Victor Colmar, Elisha Bayly, Frank Rupert, William Yost, Evans Goode.

Long may we remember P. C. Wykoff, the worthy tailor; Thomas Blake, Theodore Leckey, one of the last to go; good humored James McCullough, Sr.; Sylvester Wells and his accidental death; William Widner, our infirmary Superintendent; E. Hilbrant, frugal and industrious; I. Marks, who loved Sidney and spent his summers here; Henry Krum, the boss carpenter; Thomas Warbington, friendly, but set in his ways; George Spangler, of early lime kiln fame; Richard Mitchell, so well versed in scriptural argument; Henry Downs, full of anecdote; A. S. Robbins, the barber; the unfortunate J. L. Ayres; David Henderson; F. Grim, the father of Louis and Cyrus; John Gillespie, a patient fisherman; William A. Woolery and his team; Christian Schie, stone mason; Bennett Robbins, with his love of fine horses; William Fielding; William Sneveley, the merchant; Robert Wilson; William Day, the baker; Michael Fares, the brewer; Charles Dickerson, with his cart always on the go; Samuel Cowan, genial Doc. Deweese, and Albert Lewis, a lover of angling.

We are not forgetful of John Evans, the hotel landlord of 1868; James R. Fry, the prominent old time merchant; Daniel J. Callan, for whom the Shelby county delegation at Lima was "solid;" rare Benjamin Werst, of jovial memory; H. S. Powell, the father of Bert, of Wagner House fame; John Colford, killed a few years since on the Big Four railway; Frank Conner, who was shot accidently by a playmate at Bellefontaine; Aaron Lewis, well known; Charles Forsythe, who drowned in the cold waters of Tawawa Lake in the brightness of his youth, and Meeker Starrett, gentle and peaceable, and a genious somewhat odd.

Amos Harris was a quiet resident of the old school; Timothy Crowley was drowned; Henry Ziegler buried many Sidney people; Theoderick Randolph, a well known Negro, full of Bible quotations; Jacob Young, the father of the Young Brothers; William Johnston, once a County Commissioner and prominent farmer. A most familiar figure -- James Peebles. Who will not remember his jolly humor and kindly ways?

Thomas E. English, who came to Sidney in 1820 and died in 1876, an honorable and conscientious pioneer; Louis Weingartner, the long-time proprietor of the Union House; Andrew Maguire; James Ronan who had a pleasant word for all; James B. Laird, pike builder, and afterward Indian farm agent; James G. Brown, who died in Missouri; John Shaw, stately and straight in spite of his years; Frank Johnston, called from life in the West; William Alfele, the jovial Billy, not to be soon forgotten; Irvin Nutt, a Christian man without reproach; Julius Foust, poor Julius, who died so sorrowfully; William Pence, another life that went out untimely; Lewis Mathers, the genial and respected Cashier of the Citizens Bank, whose loss was deeply felt; venerable George Murray, our Postmaster, who threw in a cheerful word with every letter; Dr. Goode, the father of William H. C. Goode, strong and upright to the last; Colonel John Fry, the dashing soldier and progressive merchant; John Wilson, greatly respected, after whom our J. W. Conklin was named; Harry Thorne, a drummer, who well served his country, and Robert, his brother, a hotel clerk whom every body liked; James Hale, son of M. C. Hale, a young man of great probity; Walter Cromer, a young man who was connected with the Big Four railway, rapidly advancing to the highest position; Armstead Jones, who had the esteem of all; John Altermott, a most worthy and quiet German resident; Seneca Hale, whose name recalls an honored and deserving townsman; James Skillen, a son of Uncle Billy Skillen, who over-exerted himself in putting out a forest fire near Anna and died from the effects; Patrick Collins who was full of genuine Irish wit, and John Hale, honored by his county and industrious; Captain William A. Stewart, once of the regular army, was a well remembered character in Sidney, reserved and melancholy. He ended his life by jumping into the Chicago river; James Rogers had an unfortunate fall from the court house portico; Jerry Doolin was killed in his vocation on the railway; John Rice was a mercantile clerk here of most pleasant memory; Dick Burnett is gladly remembered as a young man of fine qualities, who "welcomed the coming and sped the parting guest" at the Burnett House; John Sharp for years was our gunsmith, and a nice, quiet old man; a man of strong opinions was David Flinn; Samuel Shaw was a long-lived United

Presbyterian, and financially remembered his church at his death; Preston Stewart was an energetic pusher through life, and greatly respected; Henry Harrison moved to Sidney from his farm, and died here. He was a great reader, and well posted in literature.

OBSERVATIONS, CHIDINGS AND OPINIONS

An early report lists Robert Henry Trego as the publisher of *The Sidney Journal*. He was the business manager, the keeper of the financial records and the overseer of the myriad responsibilities attendant to the production of the weekly newspaper. William (no middle name) Binkley functioned as the editor, responsible for the collection and composition of news and the writing of editorial columns that expressed the opinions of not only the newspaper owners, but also, it was hoped, of its subscribers.

Robert, a native of Bucks County, Pennsylvania, made acquaintance with William, a native of Berks County, Pennsylvania when both were young men. Together, they learned the basics of journalism while on the payroll of the *Doylestown Democrat*, a borough newspaper published north of Philadelphia. They gained additional experience under the tutelage of the editor of the *Bucks County Intelligencer*.

Armed with rudimentary knowledge of the printers' trade, William left this early employment to seek his fortune. Traveling west, he traversed the Appalachian Mountains and descended on the glacially scoured farmlands of the Buckeye State. Settling for a short period of time in Urbana, he met and married Elizabeth Hannah Chapple, a native of Devonshire, England. Another uprooting took William and his bride further west to Sidney, where he met up with his old friend Robert Trego. Together, they purchased the assets of *The Sidney Journal*, effective July 9, 1869.

Binkley was a loquacious man whose writings -- direct, succinct, sometimes flowery, often with edge and bite but always worthy of note -- were occasionally so elaborate as to almost require translation into workaday English that could be understood by the conventional reader. His reporting, of a grammatical style and spelling unique among his peers, contained neither delays nor ditherings and ranged from the extraordinary to the mundane. No item of interest seemed too small or too indecisive to include in the columns of his newspaper. He had a mission and felt a responsibility to orient that mission to the betterment of the region occupied by the readership of *The Sidney Journal*.

For 36 years Robert Trego published and William Binkley edited their weekly paper. The essence of their careers -- their personalities, their decided Republican Party leanings and their hopes for the future of the community -- remain preserved in the words and columns of the more than 1800 editions that they delivered between 1869 and 1905.

The following observations, chidings and opinions, taken verbatim from selected pages of *The Sidney Journal*, are reflective not only of a long-standing and highly successful partnership, but also of a time and lifestyles long gone, when the world was smaller, families were larger, the seasons were measured by the movement of the sun, and life, in Sidney and Shelby County, as elsewhere, had not yet been ratcheted up to the fanatical modes of the 20th century.

OBSERVATIONS

The season for cheap eggs, which usually comes every year, has passed, so from henceforth the market will have an upward tendency. Come to think about it, did not the season give us the go-by this year? Ten cents a dozen, or three for a quarter, is about the cheap limit, but they did not reach a penny apiece even in April or May, the banner months for hen fruit. Fifteen cents a dozen was the low water mark, and the price at that figure was provokingly temporary. With ham at twenty-two cents by the slice, and eggs in proportion, a person, if he lives at all, lives high. If light diet promotes health, the rising generation ought to develop into so rosy a race of robusters as to put half the doctors on their uppers. (8-5-1904)

§ § § §

The ground hog saw his shadow on Monday, and, from the present state of the thermometer, with the cold weather signed up, he was wise in seeking the seclusion of his hole. We have had free trade with Canada in wind and temperature all winter. It is about time for Congress to put a prohibitory tariff on its crossing our northern borders. If the climate of the United States was exclusively of our own manufacture there would be no 20 degrees below zero, for the Gulf States would modify the rigor of the North and the North give tonic to the South, establishing a delightful average; but, as it is, with 3,000 miles of British austerity, stretching to the frozen ocean, we are overcome, completely overwhelmed. Petitions are in order to have an embargo placed on British wind, which was always adverse to America, whether it blew from Parliament or Hudson Bay. (2-5-1885)

§ § § §

Fresh fish, lettuce and radishes from the south, and onion tops, slightly blanched at the base, are in the markets. Chickens are bursting the shells, hens are clucking, iced cream has supplanted oysters, and sun hats are doffing. Dandelions have symptoms of blooming, greens are sought for, pickles are relished, and the unmistakable spring fever is prevalent. Those who had it the hardest last year have got it the hardest this year, for it is unlike any other fever -- once having it does not grant an immunity from its repetition. It seems to abide permanently in the system when it once gets in. The crop of berries and grapes is not promising, for the vines do not look more than half alive. The ice wagons and sprinkling carts are out. Milk sours, which ensures a meal of flannel cakes in every economical household, quite as often as desired, although it is eaten without a murmur, to save the sour milk -- pigs are not allowed in town. How beautiful is spring, and yet it has its hateful features. It is invariably accompanied with house cleaning, carpet shaking, stove moving, whitewashing, etc., etc., so that, after all, it is about as vexatious as any other season, but it is here, with its pleasures and annoyances. (4-24-1885)

§ § § §

Christmas was very lively in Sidney. More and better holiday goods were sold than ever before in the same time. The display for the week previous was very attractive. Graceful trimmings and evergreen decorations lent additional charms, and no one could restrain from making purchase, though he had no friends to make glad by a gift, or stockings in his own household to fill. The weather was cold. The rain and sleet of the previous day had frozen, slippery side up, and he who attempted pedestrian elegance, did so at the expense of secure footing, and lost both grace and balance simultaneously. The book, jewelry and confectionary stores had enormous trade. M. L. Hall and clerks, who kept count, made 654 sales and wrapped up 920 packages. The saloons were crowded until far into the night, and debauchery played a full hand. (12-26-1879)

§ § § §

The bicycle is fast passing away. It is yearly coming to be less and less in demand. While it was thought some years since it had come to stay, it must now be acknowledged that it was only a fad, pure and simple, and it has gone to the place where all fads, good and bad, are sure to go. In 1895 there were 300 bicycle factories in the United States, producing annually 500,000 machines, costing the users $37,500,000 each year, and the supply was not equal to the demand. In 1896 nearly 800,000 machines were manufactured, but the price declined 40 per cent in the next two or three years, and the supply was in excess of the demand. In 1898 the membership of the League of American Wheelmen was 103,000: now it is little more than 5,000. The same year there were fifty newspapers devoted to cycling; now there is only one. So the record might be further quoted to show the gradual, but sure, decadence of interest in the use of the two wheeled vehicle. Enough has been said to establish the fact. (5-8-1903)

§ § § §

The warm and pleasant spring weather of the past few days had given a decided increase to the already large number of men and boys who seem to have nothing in the world to do except to hold up lamp posts and corner buildings, obstruct doors, hold down dry goods boxes, and make themselves nuisances generally. As the spring season opens up, there is work for all who desire it, and there is not excuse for idleness. (3-28-1879)

§ § § §

You can not catch a weasel asleep, is an old saying, but Willoughby Stewart thinks that it is easier to do than to catch one awake, for he has tried it. Yesterday morning he heard a commotion among his chickens, and, with his family, sought the cause, which proved to be a weasel. They gave chase, and ran it to the house and into the cellar. Search was made, long and careful, but in vain. Sometime afterward his little, musically inclined daughter went into the parlor to play on the organ, when, in some way, she discovered the weasel in the instrument. She ran out, frightened, and told her parents, who proceeded to dislodge the musteline. He was surely in there, but how to get him out was the question. The organ was turned upside down, upon its side, rapped and shaken, and not until half an hour of vigorous work was he captured and killed -- and he was not asleep either. (7-3-1885)

§ § § §

It has been so long since a minstrel troupe has exhibited here that there is danger that the clattering music of bones under every shade tree and on street corners will become a lost art, for it is the urchins of the rising generation who preserve it. I remember, after attending a show, how eager I was to have a rib roast bought, not so much for the meat, but for the ribs to furnish instruments for the delectable music. How carefully I scraped and seasoned them in the sun, and how persistently I practiced my left hand so that it could perform. When the hands got bridlewise, as it were, and could perform in the manner straight work, what efforts were made to clatter them behind the back, under the legs and over the head, and with what envy the boy was looked upon who had become an expert in grotesque exhibitions. The head racking hurdy gurdy is now seldom heard, but would break out if a minstrel show should come, for boys are boys now just as they used to be and will ever be. (3-20-1903)

§ § § §

Tuesday evening, while Henry Downs the fresco artist, was walking toward town on the pike near the cemetery, bearing on his shoulder a brush pole with a bucket nicely balanced on the end, smoking his pipe and serenely contemplating the picturesque beauty around him, his pipe suddenly exploded with the force of a howitzer. At first he thought some miscreant had loaded his pipe with powder, but upon reflection he came to the conclusion he himself was the author of the mischief, for he had accidently put a cartridge into his pipe when he filled it with tobacco. Whatever may have been the cause, Henry's face presents a rueful sight and his right eye looks as if he had fought a few rounds in the prize ring. (6-20-1879)

§ § § §

Park Driscoll, of Sidney, who is attending medical lectures at Columbus, was arrested at Urbana on Tuesday for having a trunk in his possession that contained two dead persons. The bodies proved to be those of two men who recently died in the Champaign county infirmary. Driscoll had a certificate from one of his Professors for the bodies, and was released. (2-5-1885)

§ § § §

It is strange, but true, that there are vandals in Sidney and vicinity who seem to delight in marring, disfiguring and injuring trees which have been planted to add beauty and comfort to our city, and especially to damage those trees which have been set on the berme bank of the canal. It will not be long, if the trees are carefully preserved, before there will be a row of stately elms through the whole length of Sidney which will give it an enviable name throughout the country. Planted at the water's edge, they are growing with amazing rapidity, and will continue to do so. It is a sad commentary on human nature that it should be even necessary to speak or write a word of warning, coupled with a penal threat, to any one to prevent the committing of vandalism. Each tree ought to be sacred in the eyes of all, great and small. In view of the fact that injuries have resulted from hitching to the young trees, careless driving wheels against them, whittling them and the like, a most liberal reward will be paid to any one who will give information leading to the conviction of any person guilty of damaging the trees. (5-22-1903)

§ § § §

"In the spring a young man's fancy lightly turns to thoughts of love," according to Tennyson, but the distinguished poet laureate does not say anything about the condition of the tender passion in midsummer. The result of observation leads to the belief that the tender passion disappears when the thermometer exceeds eighty degrees. At all events there is a great falling off in the wedding market, and most of the clergymen have very little to do in the way of joining hands and collecting fees. The young gentlemen are not particularly anxious to escort the damsels to places of amusement when the temperature is excessive, and it is not easy work to sit in a parlor with a black coat on your back and say sweet things and be polite and voluble while you are perspiring like a water cooler. Courting is out of fashion from May to October, and of course nobody wishes to be otherwise than in fashion, whether in dress or customs. (6-16-1871)

§ § § §

Saturday morning, one of those charitably disposed fellows who sell five dollars for three, drove into town, and soon his mellifluous voice was heard in the streets announcing his mode of charity. Several sales were made, and he was about ready to pull those who were nibbling at larger baits, when the officers informed him the climate was healthier a few miles up the pike. He left town considerably out of pocket. (4-4-1879)

§ § § §

An enterprising firm in Cincinnati, recognizing the strength of the public demand, has commenced the manufacture of whiskey from garbage, potato peelings, street-sweepings and the refuse of slop barrels. The product is commended by the local customers as of superior quality. As such it will soon be offered to the thirsty public. (7-22-1869)

§ § § §

Yesterday a large party from here went picnicking in the vicinity of Lockington. The heads of families took their children, and a delightful day was passed in "God's first temple." In the afternoon a party, not heads of families, but single heads, chartered the boat -- not Congressman -- General Ben. LeFevre, and went down the canal to the picnic grounds. The boat and party did not return until after 10 o'clock. In their hilarious glee, Bonnie Zinn, one of the party, fell overboard. The water was over her head, and she was powerless to rescue herself. Here was an opportunity for the young men to exhibit their gallantry and bravery. Gallantry and valor were there, and though it cost a pang to plunge their immaculate linen in the turbid waters, Frank Amann yielded to the humane impulse and plunged in, followed by Finley Cowan. Every body was saved, and but three suits water soaked. It is said that other young men would have braved the deep if it had not been for their exquisite apparel. As there were two rescuers, it is not likely that the usual matrimonial denouement will be the result. (7-13-1879)

§ § § §

About a thousand people congregated on the Miami River, below Sidney, on last Sunday, to witness the baptizing of recent converts to the church near Plattsville. It was a beautiful day, and people were present from all parts of the county. Ten persons, male and female were baptized. (4-7-1871)

§ § § §

St Valentine's day is at hand. The shop windows are full of ludicrous and ridiculous caricatures of all the professions and avocations of life, and a verse or more of the cheapest satirical doggerel accompany them. When we were a boy the day was seized upon to send a gushing token to the favored one of the opposite sex. To send one of these hideous caricatures was an intentional insult, and was taken as such by the one who received it. We used to hoard our scanty pennies for months previous to the day in order to purchase as chaste, pretty and touchingly affectionate a valentine as possible, and invariably sent it to our idol, our veritable Dulcinea Del Toboso. We, of course, disguised our handwriting, and yet felt a secret chagrin if the fair recipient failed to find out that we sent it. Her suspicions were generally correct, for previous conduct on our part had led her to suppose we were an admirer, and if she had not too many of that kind, she could with considerable precision fasten upon the author. If she failed at first, we

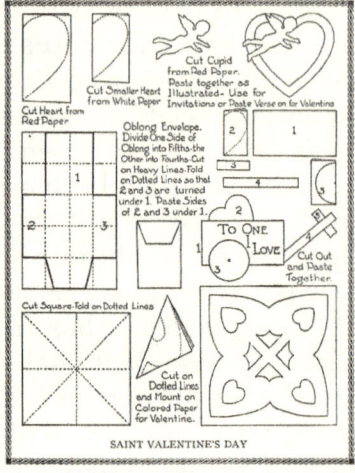

SAINT VALENTINE'S DAY

managed, by of course not intentional manifestations, to place her right in the matter. It would not do to spend one, two or three dollars on an exquisite souvenir of affection and have some one else reap the benefit. A benefit it was for almost invariably the supposed author stood on a vantage ground over all his rivals, and basked in the sunshine of nine-tenths of all her smiles. Many years ago, in a remote district in the country, when we were young, modest, and with a heart as tender as the well blanched celery tip, we melted in the presence of one we will call Laura. We went to the same district school, we were in the same class, we laughed and played and slid down hill together, and washed each other's faces in the snow. Never in life is a hoyden half so bewitching as when the returning blood comes bounding to her snow washed cheeks, and her eyes sparkle through the misty veil of disheveled hair. One day her parents moved away to another part of the country, and took this light of our school and our heart with them. What silent grief wrung us. The seat she once occupied was not half so vacant as the aching void in our heart. We were too young, too modest to give vent to our seething emotions. On her ear never fell from our lips one word that betrayed the real current of our feelings. We would have given a world to have had her know them, yet we would not for the world try to express them. So she went away with only a faint suspicion of our regard. We did not inaugurate a correspondence, but when St. Valentine's day came, sent her a costly Valentine, with a picture of arrow pierced hearts, and a chubby, curled haired cupid. We searched Byron for the most fervid outburst of amatorial passion, and in an undisguised hand inscribe it thereon, and sent it. What halcyon calm came over us when the mail started with this precious missive. Of course, she would know who sent it, and kindred feelings would be awakened in her heart, and ere long some recognition of its arrival would be received by us. We waited in vain. Was it lost? No; but far better had it been lost. In her conjectures as to who sent it, she fixed upon another, a rival of ours, and sent him her warmest acknowledgements. He did not disabuse her mind, but took advantage of it, to farther ingratiate himself in her affections. We being in agonizing ignorance he succeeded in our complete discomfiture. It was years before we found it out. We had made other arrangements then, and so had she. We have never sent another one. The instruction of this harrowing tale is evident. Do not send a costly, gushing Valentine, unless you give some unmistakable indication that you sent it or you may lose not only your Valentine, but establish some other fellow in the spot you would fain occupy yourself. (2-14-1879)

CHIDINGS

The reward is too liberal. Not that we have any fears that any one can avail himself of the reward, for that is an impossibility, but because we do not care five cents about any thing the editor may say. He uses epithets because they are his only stock in trade. His defense of any cause would be damaging to that cause. His paucity of ideas compel him to resort to blackguardism. Without this he would lapse into hopeless bankruptcy. The idea of our "squealing" -- he spells it with two e's -- on the street about his personal attack on us must have originated in his dreams, or else some one has been imposing upon the credulity of Sleepy Hollow. We are tired of repeating "editor of the *Democrat*," so from henceforth we shall call him by this synonym. We may sometimes call him Sleepy, and, perhaps, sometimes Hollow, for short, but be it understood we have reference to Sleepy Hollow, the editor of the *Democrat*. Whenever we hear any thing complimentary said of Sleepy by any Democrat we shall cheerfully give it a place in our columns; yes, we will stereotype it and keep it before the people in every issue. We have listened in vain for one for over two years. Could not some unscrupulous Democrat be hired to do violence to his feelings and send us a complimentary sentiment? But we shall not crowd our paper -- it would exclude all other matter -- by publishing the uncomplimentary remarks universally made about Sleepy by the Democrats. (8-1-1879)

§ § § §

In last week's *Democrat* there are sixteen announcements of candidates, in which the words "suitable," "satisfactory" &c., occur with pleasing frequency; and each announcement is signed "Many Democrats." Now the question is how many is many, numerously speaking? We draw the line under the column and added them up according to our arithmetic, and to save our lives we couldn't make more than sixteen in the aggregate. Then for further proof we began at the top and added downward and got sixteen again. Then we began in the middle and added upward and downward both at once and got sixteen. Then we boiled them all down, and ran them through a sieve, precipitating the whole with quicksilver, and the inevitable sixteen continued to turn up. But bear in mind that this is no possible insinuation that each candidate wrote his own notice, however it may seem to a gentleman up a stump with a forty-horsepower microscope, at all, at all. (3024-1871)

§ § § §

The mud turtles in the Miami river, Turtle creek, Loramie and tributaries are thinking about calling a convention to consider ways and means for self protection. Being in the mud most of the time, with moss on their backs, they are by nature Democrats. For the past 25 years they have been clamoring for a change in administration because now and then one would be beheaded for soup. They clamored, for they had heard in the hoop pole region, around about the reservoir, that if the Democrats got into power times would be so prosperous that no turtle would be forced out of his shell for gustatory purposes. Well, last fall the change came, with its promised prosperity. All through the winter they hugged the mud in delectable contemplation of the pleasure they would enjoy the coming summer, basking in perfect security on the banks, or coasting on the slippery rocks unmolested, while every body got fat, sleek and happy under Democratic rule. The inaugural ceremonies took place, and, as soon as the weather would permit they came to the surface to survey the new order of things. As the skirmishers among the turtles -- the advance exploring guard -- did not return to report, those still in the mud wondered at their long absence. Could it be that everything was so lovely that they had become weaned from old associations, or had some accident befallen them? While engaged in serious thought, then, bony fingers were felt clutching at their tails, and they were forcibly snaked out of their haunts and turned upon their backs in the roiling sun. The nether side of every stone

which afforded a hiding place was investigated; sharpened irons, by scores of Democratic lancers, perforated every square foot of mud and pierced their shells; tempting morsels, that concealed turtle hooks, were tossed to them, and, in fact, it seemed as if all the appliances of extermination were turned against them by Democrats, hungrier and more idle than they had ever been before. Turtles are hawked about the streets by the wash tub and wheel barrow full. This is the wholesale trade, while small boys, hanging to turtle tails, keep up the retail business. Turtle soup is not longer a rarity, but it is thrown in with a cigar or glass of beer. Fried turtle is usurping fried chicken, and a general onslaught is making all along the line. This alarming state of affairs, so different from what was promised, is the reason that a convention is contemplated. Every pledge had been forfeited. Nothing has come to pass as anticipated, and they feel gulled and more than anxious to return to the days of comparative security under Republican rule. Well, the turtles are not alone in disappointment. Those higher in the scale than this amphibian are considering and losing faith in Democratic promises and the good times coming. More fellows will be hunting turtle and skirmishing around for turtle eggs if Democratic good times continue. Even craw fish will do well if they escape. (7-10-1885)

§ § § §

Several years ago a Shelby county official asked the Auditor of Logan county what they paid their editor for printing the Assessor's blanks. The reply was, six dollars a ream. The Shelby county official then remarked that they paid their printers twenty dollars a ream. In Miami county the pubic printing amounted to some eleven hundred dollars last year. In Champaign to some nine hundred dollars. In Shelby to some nineteen hundred dollars, and was quite reasonable to what it has been during former years. Still the editor of the *Democrat* bawls for more. Did anybody ever before see one so greedy? Would it not be a good idea to levy one mill on every dollar of valuation in the county for the special benefit of said editor. Would that be enough? (5-5-1871)

§ § § §

Supposed questions put to applicants for Government positions: Do you write a good hand, and can you forge a signature adroitly and expertly? Have you ever been in the penitentiary for forging? Are you expert in covering up your tracks when guilty of embezzlement? Did you ever commit felony, from stealing a pup up to robbing an express train? Were you ever a member of the Ku Klux Klan, a night rider or soldier in the Confederate service? Did you ever stuff the ballot box, prevent Republicans from exercising offensive partisanship in the act of voting? Did you ever, when Marshal, police or Constable arrest negroes on election day without warrant or specific charges, shut them up in jail until election was over and then turn them out without a trial? If so, write the word "yes" after each question, and get a certificate of good character from the Democrats where you have lived. This latter is easily done. An affirmative answer will ensure an appointment. We want experts, for there is no telling what you may be required to do, as this is a reform Administration. (9-25-1885)

§ § § §

PASSAGES

When will editors understand their duties, or when will they have courage to perform them when they are known? It is certainly not the duty of an editor to nominate candidates for offices, or endeavor to do so. This is an abominable habit, and is too freely indulged in either for the credit of the newspaper business or the purity of politics. Of course, an editor has a right to personal preferences, but he should not be unremitting in his efforts to present such preferences through his paper. It is his duty to lay the names of all candidates before the people, and if he has reason to believe that the nomination of any one among the number would be detrimental to the interests of the public, and injurious to the party, it is his unquestioned right to oppose such nomination by all honorable means. Further than this he should not meddle with nominations through the influence of his paper. We observe a disposition on the part of certain editors in this State to nominate a candidate for Governor before the meeting of the State Convention, and a great deal of balderdash is wasted in this direction. If the same efforts were used to keep demagogues in the background, it will be impossible to get anything but a nomination acceptable to the people. We believe that such will be the case in any event, and shall be greatly surprised if some broken down politician or defunct Congressman gets the nomination. Such a calamity is possible, but barely probable. (5-12-1871)

OPINIONS

There is another thing which may well be spoken of in this connection. A commercial or mercenary feature has become manifest in the multiplicity of school books, printed in almost endless variety and foisted upon the public. The school book publishing houses are mammoth concerns and rich beyond all reason. Their oily tongued representatives infest the lobbies of all State Legislatures, they are on hand at very educational gathering and institute, and they besiege school boards and tickle them with gratuitous copies of their books, of whose merit the board has neither time to investigate, even if competent to do so. By their insinuating grace they get good books taken out of curriculum of studies, and often times inferior ones substituted, which is an especial hardship on the laboring man of the family. The movement, so universal, against these abuses will work the much needed reform and restore us to first principles. (3-20-1903)

§ § § §

A most disgraceful affair took place at Martin's beer garden, south of town, on Sunday a week ago. A young woman of Orange township, whose name we have been unable to learn, went there and drank beer with some of the young men who congregate there every Sunday, and became beastly intoxicated. She made an indecent exposure of her person, and loaded the air with blasphemy and obscenity, all to the amusement and delight of the young men and boys who happened to be there. It was an outrageous case, and should receive attention. (10-24-1879)

§ § § §

The Berea pavement walks to the court house and around it are finished; and they are wide, smooth and as nice as can be. They are made to walk on, and yet it seems that many persons have not yet found that out. The Commissioners are trying to make a beautiful lawn of the yard. Rich soil has been spread over the surface and grass seed sown several times. It is growing finely, and in a year or two there will be tough sod over it all, if not ramped to death by blundering, careless vandals. One would suppose that it would be difficult to find a single person so lost to all sense of propriety as to step on the tender blades of grass in the yard, which is so soft with the recent rains, but there are hundreds of them, male and female. The former ought to get an application of cat-o-nine-tails, and the latter hugged by a cinnamon bear until their cracking ribs made them squeal, if such a thing were possible. Last night the band gave a delightful free concert from the north balcony. The walks around the square are near enough to hear the softest strains, and yet scores went clear to the court house, tramped the grass and left prints of their odorous feet in the yielding earth. A person guilty of such carelessness ought never to hear any thing but his own cracked voice, nor see any thing but a gutter. (7-21-1885)

PASSAGES

§ § § §

If anything is responsible for the light attendance upon baseball contests it is the senseless rooting from so many of the spectators. Insulting remarks to the visiting players, attempts to perpetrate the sorriest wit, repetition of blatant would be jokes, loud flings bordering on vulgarity, if not obscenity, in which small boys take a lively hand, are intolerable to gentlemanly and womanly instincts, and, rather than submit to the positive annoyance, they stay away from the game. Just how the nuisance got a foothold is not apparent, but if it be not fatal to the National game the writer is much mistaken. Applause for good plays is all right, but a ticket of admission does not carry with it the right to be a nuisance. (5-22-1903)

§ § § §

On Wednesday John Ellis and a companion, both of Logan county, attempted to cross the Miami river at the Popular street ford. The thick ice had just broken and formed a gorge a short distance below, damning the river and raising the water. Before he got midway of the river the horses had to swim, and the wagon bed and hind wheels floated off down the stream with the companion, while Ellis clung to the front wheels and reins. He turned his team around and was drawn to the shore. The uncoupled bed struck a large cake of ice, upon which the man jumped, and was rescued by a boat. The bed, containing an overcoat, some groceries and a jug of whiskey, was drawn under the ice and lost. Dry clothing was furnished the men by Mrs. John Holder and E. J. Wagner. It was a perilous and needless affair, and reprehensible in its cruelty to animals. (3-6-1885)

§ § § §

The *Journal* believes in fair treatment; but it also believes in fair dealings. It has not joined in the popular clamor against the Miami Valley Gas and Fuel Company, but was willing at all times to give it its just dues and an impartial hearing. The word "corporation" frequently inflames the public mind without cause, and lends to rashness and injustice -- against this *The Journal* has consistently stood. The Company has, however, taken advantage of the leniency with which Sidney has regarded it, and has given the town treatment which can no longer be tolerated. In its nature it is essentially a trust, or combination, and it has exercised its power to abuse its privileges. The absorption of the Sidney Gaslight Company, and its offshoot, the Sidney Electric Light Company, by the Dayton Natural Gas Company, some years ago, was considered to be wise on the score of economy and efficiency, but since, the reorganization of the later named concern, under the title of the Miami Valley Gas and Fuel company -- a reorganization in which the stockholders were left in the outer darkness -- there has been a change in the methods of management, the sole idea being apparently, to get as much as possible and to give as little as might be in return. Consequently, the different plants have not been maintained in a proper state of efficiency, and devices have been employed which are downright dishonest -- all with a view to leave little or nothing behind in the way of property when the gas field gives out, but to take away a very considerable share of the money circulating in the Miami valley. The following facts, all of which can be established, are a sufficient basis for these charges: The Sidney Electric Company, under its management, uses the cheapest and most inferior grade of carbons, and the light it furnishes is considerably below the 2,000 candle power of its contract.

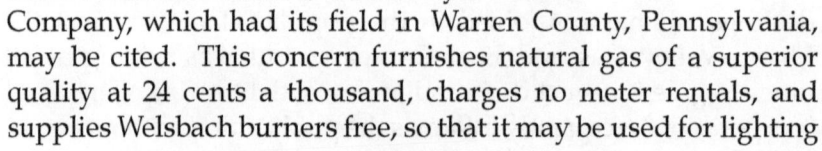

The natural gas supplied is of the most inferior quality. Oil is permitted to flow in the pipes, along with the gas, causing a great decrease in the heating quality. Moreover, the meter rentals constitute a most iniquitous imposition, as, the meters do not cost much, and most of them have in this manner paid for themselves two or three times over. As a contrast, the Pennsylvania Gas Company, which had its field in Warren County, Pennsylvania, may be cited. This concern furnishes natural gas of a superior quality at 24 cents a thousand, charges no meter rentals, and supplies Welsbach burners free, so that it may be used for lighting purposes. Worst of all, however, is the management of the Sidney Gaslight Company. The plant is old and nearly worn out, so that its capacity is altogether insufficient for the demands put upon it. There are not enough retorts to make the gas, and the coal used is about the worst which could be bought, being largely slack and full of slate. The material used to purify the gas, moreover, instead of being lime, the proper purifier, is a mixture of sawdust, iron borings, copperas and sal ammoniae, known as iron sponge -- as cheap as it is bad. All these things show dishonesty of purpose; but the worst yet remains to be told. Ever since the Miami Valley Gas and Fuel Company has had control of the Sidney Gaslight Company it has been turning natural gas at various times into the holder. At first this was not done so frequently, but in the last year or two it has been a continuous practice. For awhile a meter was put on, but it registered such an appalling amount of gas that it was taken off. In one month nearly 200,000 feet of natural gas were turned into the holder and sold to the people of Sidney as artificial gas at $1.50 a thousand. This custom of using natural gas is still in force, but no one is allowed in the retort room, for fear it should be discovered. A more bare faced robbery was never perpetrated. Lastly, when there was a general adjustment of the meters three years ago, they were fixed so to make many of them run faster than before, thus registering more gas. (3-26-1897)

§ § § §

"A soft answer turneth away wrath," quotes a cotemporary, and then undertakes to fortify the position by narrating an incident of boorishness on the part of a postoffice official to a patron who laid down two cents at the stamp window without saying what he wanted, and who, in response to the question, "Well what do you want: answered mildly, "An automobile, please." This is a far fetched argument for a "soft answer." The duty of public officials is to be courteous to patrons, and there is no excuse for boorishness anywhere, nor at any time, but there are always reciprocal obligations. The busy post office clerk or railway agent is asked a thousand questions each day, and it is his duty to give in return a thousand courteous answers. It is equally the bounden duty of the persons asking the questions to be polite and kindly in their bearing toward the officials. In the case quoted it was encumbent on the patron who laid down the two cents to kindly make his wants known. By what kind of telepathic instinct could the postoffice clerk know whether his customer wanted a two cent stamp, or two one cent stamps, or a stamped wrapper, or a stamped envelope. The ironical response that an automobile was wanted was the retort discourteous, and not the retort courteous. It was exactly the opposite of a soft answer. The moralizing of our cotemporary is neither philosophical not warranted by the facts. Along the same lines of reciprocal duties are those which appertain to telephonic communications. Each user is entitled to courteous questions and answers. (1-30-1903)

§§§§

A good deal of unnecessary and uncalled for fuss was made at the Methodist church on the evening of Dr. Talmage's lecture, and is still rife, in respect to the doors into the audience room being kept closed until 7:30 o:clock. In the first place the ladies were right in keeping them closed, for they had so advertised. In the next place, they threw open the doors of the basement, where any one could comfortably sit until the time announced. There was no necessity in crowding and jamming the vestibule and stairways so that even the officers could not perform their duties. A little authority exercised by a sturdy policeman would not have been inopportune at the crisis. Every criticism upon the matter is unjust, peevish and petulant, and reflects no credit on the preeminently selfish fault finders. Talmage drew the largest audience . . . that ever turned out in Sidney to hear a lecture. Curiosity to see the lecturer more than any thing else drew the large audience. Some points were exceedingly well put, but many were not worth the time occupied in giving them. He is addicted to slang. It may pass for wit among corner loafers, but it is unpardonable in a man who occupies the position and makes the pretentions Talmage does. He may design his antics on the platform as fine acting, but the average person will take them to be gyrations and calisthenics exercises. (3-20-1885)

§ § § §

Last year the *Journal* advised the farmers of Shelby county not to plant excessively of the edible tubers when seed was worth $1 and upward a bushel, as at least $10 worth of seed would be required for each acre, and the high price last year would induce farmers to plant a large acreage, which would inevitably make the price low this spring. Still, a large acreage was planted, and potatoes go begging at twenty-five and thirty cents a bushel, much less than could have been got last fall. The probability is that it will pay far better to plant them this season than last, and it may be pertinent to give a resume of what a large raiser of potatoes said at a horticultural meeting in Indiana not long since. Plow, plant, cultivate, fight bugs and dig. Soil which will produce corn or straw will produce potatoes. Plow eight inches deep and stir the soil every week. Harrow after each rain, and often. Mark deep, and plant six inches deep, a foot or more apart in the row. Cover with a spike-tooth harrow. Have the rows three and one-half feet apart. After the vines are up cover them with soil: it kills weeds and eggs. Use large, well matured potatoes for seed. Cut the seed ten days before planting and expose them to the sun, as it will kill the scab, and get seed from the North if you have to buy; it is well to change seed. Well rotted stable manure is the best fertilizer. Frequent stirring of the surface of the soil is absolutely essential. (4-24-1903)

§ § § §

About sixty persons accompanied the excursion from Sidney to Lima, last Sunday, to visit the encampment of the Eleventh Regiment Ohio National Guards. The sham battle did not take place, the notable men advertised to be present were not there, and the people were disappointed. Drunkenness and ruffianism held sway, and the sanctity of the day and all rules of decorum were ruthlessly violated. Returning, a number of roughs from the vicinity of Wapakoneta fought on the train, no less than three knockdowns and half a dozen scuffles occurring on one car. (9-12-1879)

§ § § §

It is dense ignorance and absurd presumption to assume that any one particular religious organization has a monopoly of the truth, and all others are only imitators, or that one has the divine sanction exclusively, and all others are but human institutions. The fact is they are all human institutions. There is not revealed authority for any of them. They are all traditionary, yet all have divine sanction. They are all the results of the development of the truth as originally promulgated, but not one is authorized by the truth to the exclusion of all the rest. The institutional feature of them is necessary to the highest order of mechanical success, but not to the clearest conception of abstract truth. When the institution idea becomes subordinate then sectarian walls will tumble, and energies now wasted in polemic warfare will be directed into channels of help for suffering mankind. The trend is that way now. (3-6-1903)

§ § § §

The contract for the new iron bridge across the canal on Main street, and the removal of the old one to Berlin, has been let to E. Anderson & Sons without advertising for proposals. No one knows the price or the terms of the contract, if there is any. When has there been a bridge letting? Not for nearly two years. E. Anderson & Sons are privately awarded all jobs. Now, *The Journal* has no objections to E. Anderson & Sons, but it has objections to this system of transacting the business of the county. It is illegal; it is extravagant; it is dishonest; it is unjust to the taxpayers; it is favoritism in its worst phases. This system obtains in every department of our county affairs, and costs the people thousands of dollars. (6-27-1879)

§ § § §

As there is to be no fence around the square, it is suggested that the Commissioners put up a hand rail for the benefit of the ladies who walk on the coping. A recital of a few of the numerous cases that have plunged head foremost on to the gravel walk are in order to prove that a hand rail or an escort ought to be furnished. A nicely dressed lady, one of the first, cast her eyes upward to view the town clock, walked a few steps, lost her bearing, and landed a la quadruped in the square. Another recognized a friend across the street, bowed her head, and then made two dimples in the gravelly walk with her knees. Another, with her umbrella, was caught in a sudden gust, and, after a moment of earnest, but vain, effort to keep her balance, dove into her concave protector against rain, played smash with the whalebone, and sprained her finger. These are sufficient to show the need of protection. (4-10-1885)

§ § § §

Some strictures have been passed on officer Jacob Wagner for misconduct on the night of the election. Mr. Wagner did no more than his duty, and it was well for the Democratic hoodlums around the Republican headquarters that he did order them away, and also that they went away. The Republicans were becoming indignant, and soon would have clothed themselves with official authority and have dispersed the rabble. This is not the first time that disturbances of this kind have occurred, but we warn these disturbers not to attempt anything of the kind again, or trouble will ensue. (10-24-1879)

§ § § §

Worse than whiskey and money for electioneering purposes is the appeal to nationality and religion. When a man becomes a citizen of the United States he has no business to base any demands for place or position upon the fact that he is Irish or German born. About ten years ago religious clannishness began to show itself in politics in Shelby county, and it has developed alarmingly ever since. The claim that such a man should be nominated because he can carry his church ought to be tramped out. (4-17-1885)

§ § § §

Firms employing traveling men generally have honorable gentlemen on the road. The Auburn Glove and Mitten

Manufacturing Company, Auburn, New York is an exception. Frank P. Dunn, representing the concern, was in Sidney last week, and during the short time he was here succeeded in establishing himself as a shyster of no mean proportions. (6-27-1879)

§ § § §

The Board of Health, although largely composed of physicians, is really getting down to business, and is doing excellent work. It believes that an ounce of prevention is worth a pound of cure, and, though it has been distressingly healthy here and in the region about, that is distressingly for it, it is nobly putting its shoulder to the wheel, taking all the noxious outposts and putting them in defensive repair against malaria, cholera infantum and cholera adultum. It has employed a health policeman to ferret out, investigate and report unsavory places, and then it issues notices on the proprietors of the offensive nosegays to abate the nuisances, or fumigate them to the approval of the nicest attuned olfactories. Pig pens are doomed in Sidney. They must go, like offensive partisans, and the occupants yield up their oleaginous bodies and be resolved into spare rib, sausage, souse, head cheese, wienerwurst, ham shoulder and breakfast bacon. Well, a hog is rightly named, and he has no business in a Christian town. The four legged ones can be reached by ordinance, and after they are all excommunicated there will still be enough of the biped order dodging around to preserve the stock, do the rooting and devour the soured fruit -- the job lots. It is not likely that anything but the most flagrant, fragrant places will be turned up topsy-turvy this year, but next year odorous feet of long standing, body effluvia of long sweating, discolored teeth, with their debris of long accumulation, will come under the ban of its displeasure, and even foul breath receive a passing notice, with chloride of lime suggestions. We are going to have a clean, healthy town, even if every doctor has to be put on the charity list; that is the cheapest way to keep them, anyhow, and Graceland cemetery has to be content with now and then a tough morsel of four score years and upward. It is said that steam whistles provoke catalepsy, epilepsy, insomnia, softening of the brain, tympanum difficulties, moral decay and rickets, and, if this can be made to appear, they will be made to use rubber tubes and "roar as gently as sucking doves." O what a delightful place Sidney will be! It will smell like Araby the Blest, the Vale of Cashmere, or Ceylon's spicy isle, and no discordant hell-broke-loose shrieks split the ear. (8-7-1885)

§ § § §

What Sidney needs is a boss. Not a political boss. It has had and has them -- more than has been and is good. Any of the kind would be too many, but the city needs a man of large brain, honest heart, unselfish motives, comprehensive mind, broad views, unflinching courage, good taste, high ideals, strength of character, generous nature and the ability to do things, to come to the front and direct the interests and enterprises of the city for the next ten years. For the absence of such a man we are twenty-five years behind our possibilities. The experiences of the last two years have brought to view and emphasized our defects. Our streets and alleys, gutters and crossings, cheap wooden structures allowed to be set up on the most prominent corners, garbage heaps and closets and many other details peculiar to the physical features of communities like ours, daily proclaim the need of a master force such as has been described. There has been no uniform system of making improvements, nor of keeping up what have been made. Everything has been done by piecemeal, disjointed, disconnected and inharmonious. Men have sought places on the Councilmanic board with no other motive nor purpose than to advance some personal and local interest. One grade has been made in one street and another in another according to certain individual and Councilmanic desires, a load of gravel has been dumped here and another there, or the soil has been hauled from the streets without any kind of regard for uniformity of service or advantage, valuable franchises have been given away without restraint or restriction, sidewalks have been allowed to be impinged upon by abutting steps and verandas, street fakirs are permitted to expose all kinds of bogus shows, and auctioneers to obstruct the sidewalks with crowds for the sale of their wares, shade trees have been mutilated or cut down with impunity; but why attempt to enumerate the evils which place us below the level of the smallest village in the county in point of those things which ought to make us great? It may be answered that no one man of whatever merit could lift us to the place we are entitled to occupy. True, not in himself, but one such broad, strong, unselfish leader as has been defined would speedily find a following of men and women who would stand by and support him in the accomplishment of the results indicated. There are many men and women of high ideals and proper conceptions who would gladly rally to the kind of leader described. There would be a contest and severe struggle with the selfish, narrow contracted, uncouth little souls who are happy only in the atmosphere of their own kind, but the victory would be for the right things sooner or later. Is there some one who has come to the kingdom for such a work? (4-24-1903)

THE AUTHOR

Albert Binkley Dickas was born in Sidney in 1933, the son of Lionel Adrianne and Helen Binkley Dickas. His basic education was received under the tutelage of the Sisters of Charity of Cincinnati at Holy Angels Grade and High School, beginning in 1938 and graduating 13 years later as a member of the class of 1951. In subsequent years he earned BA and MS degrees from Miami University (Oxford, Ohio) and a PhD degree from Michigan State University, all in the academic fields of geology and geophysics. Industrial experiences include associations with Magnolia Petroleum Company (Mobil Oil), in the Gulf of Mexico province, and Standard Oil Company of California, in both the Bakersfield exploration office and the International Research Division facilities in Los Angeles.

Joining the staff of the University of Wisconsin - Superior, in 1966, he spent the next 31 years in a variety of activities: classroom instruction; the founding of a research center focused on environmental problems related to Lake Superior; establishment of a cooperative exchange program with Rostov State University in the USSR; authorship of more than 70 professional papers; editing of four published volumes of geological literature; and the presentation of numerous papers on the subjects of petroleum geology, worldwide Precambrian oil reserves, and comparative tectonics between the billion-year-old Midcontinent Rift System of North America and the modern rift system of East Africa. He completed his academic career as Associate Vice Chancellor for Research.

Retiring to southwest Virginia, he built a home on the crest of Brush Mountain, where he maintains interests in research, writing and travel, the latter both in this country and abroad. In his spare time attempts are made, with varying degrees of success, to keep track of the whereabouts and birthday dates of his four children and eight grandchildren.

www.ingramcontent.com/pod-product-compliance
Lightning Source LLC
Chambersburg PA
CBHW031311150426
43191CB00005B/179